by
Hollis Lee

Countryside
Books

Preface

If you own a few acres or plan to acquire a country place, you probably know about the rich rewards associated with country living: the open space, the fresh air, the chance to do some real farming, gardening and animal raising on your own land.

*We have published this series of **Country Home & Small Farm Guides** to provide the basics you'll need to succeed in a broad range of projects and activities on two acres or 100.*

We realize that for most people country living is a very private pursuit. After all, a big part of its appeal is not having to look into the next guy's window when you look out of yours. But we hope you will communicate with us. Tell us how you like our books, share bits of country wisdom and suggest additional subjects or services we can provide.

Contents

Introduction   **4**

The Orchard   **5**

The Apple   **8**

The Peach   **26**

The Nectarine   **44**

The Pear   **46**

The Plum   **56**

The Apricot   **64**

The Cherry   **70**

Dwarf Fruit Trees   **76**

Propagating Fruit Trees   **80**

Beekeeping   **87**

Glossary   **93**

Illustrations by Wayne Kibar

ISBN 0-88453-029-9

©1978 by Countryside Books
A.B. Morse Company, 200 James Street, Barrington, IL 60010

Printed in U.S.A.

Introduction

4

Apples, peaches, pears and other fruit are foods that will improve your diet and increase the appeal of your roadside market. Because of their numerous varieties, you are bound to find at least one variety of each that will grow in your area.

This book contains specific information about planning and preparation, planting, pruning, training, soil management, propagating, pollination, harvesting, insects and diseases, and varieties. These data, along with consultation with your local county agent concerning local problems, should help you raise a successful orchard, whether it is large or small.

The Orchard

The type of orchard you develop depends upon how you intend to use it. The first decision you need to make is whether the orchard is strictly for home use with possible marketing of the surplus or whether it is to be a small commercial operation.

If your orchard is for home use, plan to diversify the planting; that is, plant several varieties of different kinds of fruit trees so that the ripening periods of the fruit can be spread over a longer period of time. Nothing is more satisfying both to the palate and the ego than to walk through an orchard and pick ripe fruit off the tree. That is furnishing food for the stomach and the soul!!

Dwarf trees are becoming more popular and are worth considering. This will allow you to plant more kinds of trees and more varieties of each kind in the same amount of space. They are also normally easier to care for.

You might want to plant fruit not normally grown in your area. Sometimes such planting may produce only small amounts of fruit or a crop once every two or three years. This would still make it worthwhile if it happens to be a fruit the family would particularly enjoy. In some cases, the self-satisfaction alone would make it worth the effort.

If you are establishing a small commercial operation, it would be better to specialize in one particular kind of fruit. You should probably vary the varieties in order to spread the labor requirements and marketing potential over a longer period of time. In deciding which kind of fruit to grow for market, take into account (1) which fruit crop is best adapted to your locality and to the soils on your particular farm, (2) the cost of mechanization and labor required to plant, harvest and maintain the trees, and (3) the market outlets available for marketing the fruit.

Normally, there are three possible outlets for fruit — the fresh market, packers-distributors, and processing plants. The fresh market offers the best possibility for maximum income, but selling in this manner takes more time and often results in higher spoilage losses. Also, fresh markets in towns and small cities can easily be

5

oversupplied. A growing development in fresh fruit marketing has been the so-called "pick it yourself" trend. The success has varied somewhat, but if the location is good, the marketing results are usually very good. This type of marketing normally will offer one of the highest net incomes per unit. Packers and distributors pay less, but provide a fairly steady and reliable market. Selling to them does not take much time, and some buy the crop in the orchard and harvest it. Processing plants pay the least, but they are a more certain market. Many of them will contract the crop and provide technical help, especially with insect and disease control programs. All localities, of course, do not have processing plants conveniently available.

Your local county agent, state experiment stations and extension services will have the latest information available on new varieties adapted to the area, new techniques, insect and disease control, local spray schedule, and possible sources for nursery stock. Don't hesitate to use their services. That's what they are paid to do; in fact, their jobs depend on serving the farmers.

When making plans for an orchard, consult a reliable nurseryman, one in your vicinity if possible. He not only will know about the various varieties, but will have knowledge about what rootstock is best adapted to the area. Rootstock can be a very important factor in a successful orchard operation. A good variety will sometimes fail if it is not on the right rootstock.

Most fruit trees reproduce themselves by means of seeds, but their offspring differ widely; they must be maintained by vegetative propagation. By means of budding or grafting, two distinct parts (the root system and the stem and branch system), which may have very diverse characteristics, are made to grow together as a single plant. The best idea is to purchase your planting stock from reliable nurserymen instead of trying to grow your own. There is a considerable saving in time, and the techniques of proper propagation by budding and grafting are difficult for the layman. There may be times when you may want to try some experiments where budding or grafting is required. For that reason the methods are outlined later in the book.

The Apple

The apple is the main deciduous tree fruit in the world. Although the early history of the domestic apple has been lost, it probably originated in the South Caucasus in the Soviet Union. Before the Christian era the fruit had spread to Europe where it grew in both domestic and wild forms.

The first settlers brought the apple to the eastern United States and spread it westward as they moved across the country. John Chapman, one of the main planters and distributors of apples, gave seeds to the westward-moving families; he became known as Johnny Appleseed. By the mid-1800's the apple had become established from coast to coast.

Today the United States is responsible for approximately one-quarter of the world's apple production. They are grown in nearly every state in the Union, particularly Washington, New York and Michigan.

The improved varieties of today's apples are a far cry from the wild apples from which they developed, so much so that the taxonomy is confused. Some authorities use the scientific name *Pyrus sylvestris* while others use *Pyrus malus.* Some prefer to use the generic term Malus for the apple and restrict Pyrus to the pear. To confuse things even more, at one time or another, many different fruits have been known as apples.

Planning and Preparation

Careful planning and preparation for apple planting is time well spent and results in greater returns over the years. This is true whether you are setting out only a few trees for your own use or establishing a small commercial orchard. After all, the bearing life of apple trees should be from 30 to 50 years if properly cared for. Consider some of the following items when you are making a decision to plant apple trees.

Varieties

Select varieties well adapted to the area and region. If you are growing apples for home use, try some varieties that are not

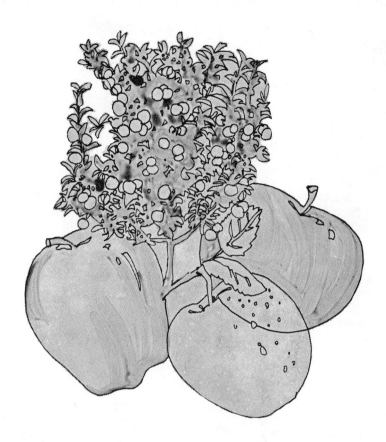

normally planted in order to extend the ripening periods and offer a wider choice of fruit.

Precipitation

Annual precipitation should be at least 24 inches well distributed over the growing season. Where irrigation is available, rainfall is less important; however, some type of irrigation is highly desirable except in the high rainfall areas.

Humidity

Disease problems are caused by high humidity during the fruiting season. Production costs often increase due to attempts at controlling fungus diseases, particularly apple scab.

Sunshine

Abundant sunshine is important to growing apples since it is largely responsible for high color in apples. Areas that are free from dust and smoke are better for apple trees.

Temperature

Apple varieties differ in their resistance to low temperatures and their response to mild winters and hot summers. Apples succeed best in areas where the trees are not exposed to wide variations in temperatures during their winter's rest.

In late summer and early fall temperature is important in developing red color. Warm days and cool nights are best. In some areas the fruit may develop satisfactorily, but lack a good high red color.

Site location

If possible, select a site on a gentle slope with low lying land at its base to which colder air may drain. This insures good air drainage through and away from the apple trees. Good air drainage not only lessens the risk from frost, but also helps avoid spread of fungus diseases.

Since the ideal location for apple trees is on slopes, consider contouring and terracing the land prior to planting the trees.

Drainage

Water drainage is a must for apple trees because they cannot tolerate "wet feet." If your location has good surface drainage except for a low spot, drain that particular area. If you construct terraces, create them with a slight fall to a waterway.

Soil

Although some varieties do better on certain soils, apples generally thrive on a wide range of soil types. The soil should be deep, 5 feet if possible, although apple trees will thrive on shallow soil. The nature of the subsoil is as important as the soil itself. The subsoil should be well drained so that the tree roots at no time stand in water. A hard impervious subsoil restricts root development, which in turn will affect the tree's life and vigor. A very open subsoil that holds little or no water is the opposite extreme.

10

Apple trees will grow on a fairly wide range of soil pH, but 6.5 to 6.8 appears to be best. If you need to make adjustments to the soil, make them a year or two in advance if possible.

The time and money you expend to build up the soil's fertility and get it into condition are a good investment. Raise a crop or two or a green manure crop on the land where you intend to plant the apple trees. This will condition the soil, allow it time to lime and fertilize properly, and give you time to correct the drainage problems that may occur.

Planting

Use the following directions when you are ready to plant your apple trees.

Preparing to plant

1. Order the trees from the nursery well in advance of planting time to insure delivery of the trees at the proper time. Plant in the spring as early as the land can be worked. Fall planting can be done in regions with comparatively mild winters.
2. If you cannot plant the trees immediately upon arrival, examine the roots.
3. If they are somewhat dry, soak them at once and keep them moist until heeled-in or planted. To heel-in the trees, dig a shallow trench in a shaded spot and cover the roots and a foot or more of the lower part of the trunk with moist soil. Keep it moist until the trees are planted. When planting, keep the roots protected because 15 or 20 minutes of dry wind will injure the roots.

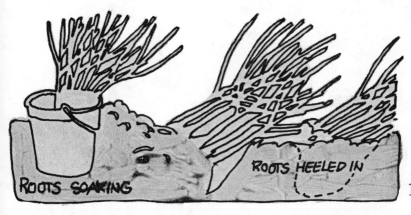

ROOTS SOAKING   ROOTS HEELED IN

11

4. Plant the apple trees on the contour or by using the square or triangular method.
5. Plan to plant them 30 to 40 feet apart, although the space will depend upon the rootstock, soil and variety.
6. After you have determined the spacing, locate a stake for each tree. Check the sightings for any stakes that might be out of line.
7. Use a planting board to set the trees. *(See following page.)*

Tree Planting Board

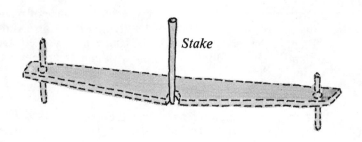

Stake

12

Planting the trees.
1. Remove the broken and extra long roots.
2. Dig a hole larger than the spread of the roots.
3. Set the tree 1 to 2 inches deeper in the hole than it grew in the nursery.
4. Use topsoil and sand to backfill the hole.
5. Use enough water to make a slurry around the roots and firm the soil around the tree.
6. Be sure to remove any air pockets around the roots.
7. Do not let the roots dry out before or during the planting operation.
8. Do not put commercial fertilizer in the hole with the roots at planting time.

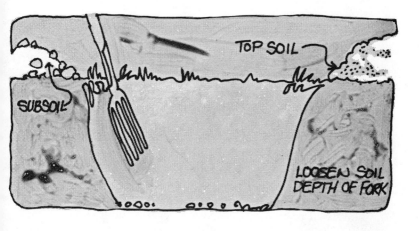

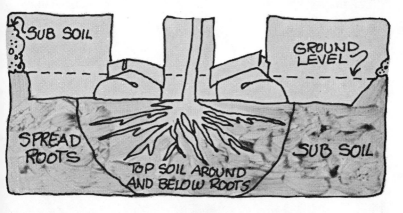

Pruning and Thinning

Pruning and thinning apple trees is a must for successful production. They're important for five basic reasons: 1) to train a young nonbearing tree so that a strong framework will develop; 2) to shape the tree within a reasonable size for harvesting, spraying, and other orchard operations; 3) to thin crops to achieve good size fruit and yield; 4) to maintain adequate shoot growth; and 5) to keep the tree reasonably open to admit sunlight and insure good aeration. This, in turn, helps promote good quality fruit, aids in ntrolling disease and facilitates thinning and picking.

A term applied to pruning fruit trees is *mold-and-hold*. This means that the frame and height of the tree are determined by formative pruning (molding) during the development period, and the form is held by regular, light corrective pruning.

Pruning at planting time

Pruning at planting time should be severe. Because it is difficult for the developing root system to support a lot of limb and leaf area, the more severe the pruning, the sooner the transplanted tree becomes established.

To insure the development of a good framework, head-back the one-year-old whip at planting time to a good strong bud at a height of about 4 feet. To head-back means to remove only a portion of the limb or branch, leaving a part from which new growth can occur. The bud below the cut will elongate and side shoots will form.

Pruning a nonbearing tree

1. If a strong branch has developed 2 to 3 feet from the ground, select it as the bottom scaffold limb.
2. Select 2 or 3 additional branches spaced at least 6 to 8 inches apart along the trunk and extending in different directions from the trunk.
3. If the top branch is weak, remove it and develop the leader from a lower, stronger growing branch. You don't need to select all the laterals the second year. Additional laterals can be developed in succeeding years.
4. You may need to debud the whip of all buds except those where the laterals are desired. This method produces a good sound framework for the continued growth of the tree.
5. If narrow crotch angles develop, remove them and train other laterals to take their place. A toothpick can be inserted between young laterals and the trunk to insure that they will develop into strong angles.

14

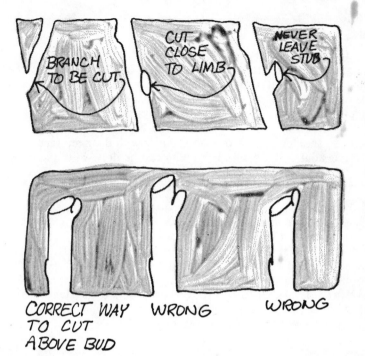

BRANCH TO BE CUT

CUT CLOSE TO LIMB

NEVER LEAVE STUB

CORRECT WAY TO CUT ABOVE BUD

WRONG

WRONG

Thinning a bearing tree

Thinning the wood and fruit on apple trees is a good orchard practice that helps to obtain a good fruit set every year. Without this thinning, apples tend to set a heavy crop one year and then bear little or no crop the next. Thinning also increases the percentage of top-grade fruit, increases the size and improves the color. It decreases preharvest fruit drop, promotes tree vigor, reduces winter injury, reduces limb breakage, and minimizes the handling of low-grade fruit.

Thinning the wood means to remove entirely a shoot, spur, branch or other part. The cut is made where these grow out from the parent stem; thus, thinning reduces the amount of branches or limbs. Thinning is necessary to open up the top to let in sunlight; heading-back makes spraying and picking more economical. Young bearing trees need very little wood removed until you can tell to what extent the top is going to open up. The fruit on young trees tends to open up the top.

Hand thinning the young fruit is the ideal method for spacing apples on the tree and at the same time eliminating potential culls. This method will probably be satisfactory if you have only a few

15

trees to thin. However, for a larger orchard, the labor and time involved makes it costly.

If you have an orchard with large numbers of apple trees, use chemical thinning with caustic sprays and auxin sprays. Apply the spray during bloom to prevent the freshly opened flowers from fertilizing. The spray induces an incompatible condition between the pollen tubes and stylar tissue. Sodium salt of naphthaleneacetic acid (NAA) and dinitro (DN) are the compounds most widely used and should be applied in accordance with the manufacturer's recommendations. Chemical thinning can be done with any good sprayer. These thinning materials are compatible with most insecticides and fungicides used in apple orchards and may be sprayed at the same time.

Apple trees are subject to preharvest fruit drop. Some trees will drop fruit throughout the entire season from calyx stage to harvest time. Generally fruit drop occurs about 6 weeks after bloom and just before maturity. The loss from preharvest drop can be serious, often amounting to as much as 50% of the crop. Sprays have been developed to control the drop period just before maturity. Fair success has been achieved with sprays of alar and ethephon, as well as a few other products.

Soil Management

The first three or four years in the life of an apple tree are very important. This is when the vigor and shape of the trees are determined. Make every effort to get the young trees established quickly so they can make good growth.

Irrigation

Do not let the young tree get stressed from the lack of water. If necessary, irrigate the trees.

Cultivation

16   Follow a system of limited cultivation for the first few years. Shallow cultivation should be done in spring during the growth period to conserve moisture by eliminating competition from weeds and to help incorporate organic matter and fertilizer into the soil. Stop cultivation in early summer.

Cover crop

Grow a cover crop to aid in hardening the trees and to provide protection for roots during the winter. The cover crop should be disked into the soil in spring to add organic material to the soil.

Herbicides

Use herbicides to control grass and weeds that grow under the trees where they compete seriously for water and fertilizer. Follow the manufacturer's directions.

Mulching

Excellent results are obtained from heavy mulching along with restricted use of chemical herbicides. If a mulch of straw, hay or other organic matter is spread around the tree to a depth of 3 inches when settled, it produces a beneficial effect on the trees in several ways. The humus content of the soil increases the moisture-holding capacity so that porosity and aeration are improved; erosion and runoff water are controlled; there is less fluctuation in soil temperatures; and nutrients are added to the soil.

Fertilizing

The amount you fertilize apple trees should be based on soil tests and leaf analysis. The relation between chemical nature of the soil and nutritional status of the tree is influenced by factors such as rootstock, pruning, injury and variety, which have no bearing on availability of soil nutrients. Trees are grown in soils varying widely in physical and chemical composition. Each different soil condition has an influence on availability of nutrients to the tree.

Apple trees in production use nitrogen and potassium in a 3 to 1 ratio with phosphorus. Any fertilizers you use should be heavy in nitrogen and potassium content.

Nitrogen

Nitrogen has the most effect on growth of the apple tree. In most soils, however, nitrogen is present only in small amounts. Unless nitrogen is available in sufficient quantities, you cannot expect a good crop of high quality apples, regardless of other factors.

Nitrogen is available in several forms. Use the one best suited to your conditions and most economical in price. Ammonium nitrate is usually available and easy to apply. Apply it at a rate of about ¼ pound per year of the tree's age to a maximum of 4 to 5 pounds per tree. Being highly soluble, you can broadcast it on the soil from the dripline in toward the trunk in the early spring just as vigorous growth is starting.

17

Phosphorus

The phosphorus requirement of apple trees is small, but this element is required in the metabolic processes. If soil tests show that the soil is deficient, add phosphates to the fertilizer program.

Potassium

Apple trees are heavy feeders of potassium, which is essential in manufacturing and translocating sugars and starches. It is also a factor in water take-up. The balance between potassium and nitrogen is very important.

Nitrogen stimulates tree growth and increases the need for potassium. This can lead to a deficiency of potassium if not corrected. Large applications of potassium do not generally do any harm and tend to stay in the soil longer than other minerals A basic rate of applying potassium sulfate is about 3-5 pounds per mature tree. Also, a spray of 1 pound of potassium sulfate mixed with 100 gallons of water applied directly to the foliage can correct potassium deficiency in the season in which it occurs.

Other elements

Apples in some locations suffer from the lack of one or more of the minor elements such as boron, magnesium, manganese, copper or zinc. Foliar sprays are the normal treatment for such deficiencies. Request recommendations from the local county agent for such treatments.

Pollination

Apple varieties, for all practical purposes, are unfruitful; that is, they require another apple variety for cross-pollination in order to set a good crop of fruit. Therefore, you need to provide suitable pollinizer varieties in the orchard. This should be done when the orchard is planted. A good rule of thumb is to have a pollinizer tree located within 100 feet of the production trees. Some varieties, such as Rhode Island Greening, produce defective pollen. Others are good pollinators, including Winesap, Stayman, and McIntosh.

Cross-pollination is achieved by insects, especially honeybees. Bumblebees will work during weather too cold for honeybees and

18

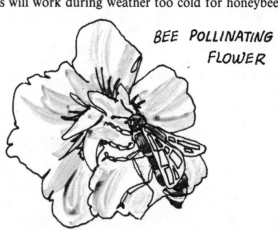

BEE POLLINATING
FLOWER

are important in some years. One good strong hive of bees should be kept for each acre of apple trees.

Climatic conditions affect pollination. Very high relative humidity prevents proper release of pollen and low humidity reduces pollen germination. Rain during bloom may wash pollen away and prevent bees from working. If the temperature stays below 50°F at pollination time, the set of fruit may be decreased. Germination is also inhibited by temperatures about 80°F. Pollen of apple and other fruit trees is heavy, so wind has very little effect.

Harvesting

Harvesting at the proper stage of maturation is very important. Apples picked while immature lack flavor and quality, tend to shrink and shrivel in storage, lack attractiveness, and are subject to disorders such as storage scald, bitter pit, and brown core. Use a combination of the following maturity indices to determine harvesting time.

1. Seed color — most apple varieties have brown seed when ready for harvest.
2. Size of fruit.
3. Skin color.
4. Firmness of flesh.
5. Separation from spur — as apples reach maturity, they tend to hold less tightly to the tree. If in picking you remove many spurs and pull out stems, the fruit has not reached proper maturity for harvest.
6. Taste — a few representative apples may provide information for decision in picking. Note that a variety may taste sweet not because the sugar content is high, but because the acid content is low.

If the apple trees have been properly pruned and shaped, an 8 foot stepladder should allow you to reach most of the fruit. Aluminum ladders, because of their strength and lighter weight, are preferable to wood. The ideal picking container protects the fruit from bruising and is easy to fill and empty. A container with rigid sides gives the most protection to the fruit. Apples bruise when squeezed, bumped or dropped 2-3 inches. Such bruises may not be immediately apparent, but will show up later to lower the quality of the fruit.

Apples remain alive even after they are picked from the tree. The length of time that apples remain good after picking varies with the stage of ripeness at picking, the length of time they remain at ordinary temperature, and the variety. The apples tend to breathe after picking, the greater the respiration, the shorter the storage life. Low temperature slows down the rate of respiration and prolongs the storage life. Low temperatures also slow down enzyme activity and inhibit the growth of rot organisms. If you want to store your apples, cool them as rapidly as possible and hold them at a temperature of about 32°F for maximum storage life. Do not let the apples freeze.

Insects

Insect and disease control for apple trees starts with a good sanitation program. Sanitation is a general control practice for pests in the orchard. Destroy hawthorns and other wild fruit trees on the property, since these host many orchard pests and diseases. Remove dead limbs and dying trees and spray any props left in the orchard. Remove culls from the orchard and bury or destroy.

Check with the local county agent for a local spray calendar. Use insecticides in strict accordance with the manufacturer's recommendations. Read all labels carefully.

Moths

The codling and bud moths are pests that cause growers a great deal of trouble. The adults are greyish-brown. The larva, or worm, is about 3/4″ long and attacks both the buds and the fruit.

Leaf rollers

The larva is a slender caterpillar that feeds on the opening leaves and eats parts of the young fruit. Second and third broods cause the most severe damage. All varieties are subject to attack, but Cortland and Rhode Island Greening are especially susceptible.

Apple maggot

The adult fly is somewhat smaller than the common house fly with a black mark on each wing. The maggot is only about 1/3 inch in length and is seldom seen until the apple is over-ripe. Two of the varieties more susceptible to the maggot are Yellow Transparent and Wealthy. McIntosh is the most resistant.

Plum curculio

The adult is a brown beetle about 1/34 inch long with a curved strong snout. The female deposits the egg in a hole eaten in the skin of the fruit. The grub develops in the skin.

Aphids

The green apple aphid is one of the most destructive. It sucks the sap from the leaves, particularly near the growing tip, and causes a sooty fungus on the fruit.

APPLE SCAB

PLUM CURCULIO

SAN JOSE SCALE

EUROPEAN RED MITE

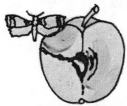

CODLING MOTH

JAPANESE BEETLE

21

APHID

APPLE MAGGOT

Mites

The European Red mite causes problems on Delicious Yellow Transparent and Early McIntosh. The mites suck the sap from the leaves and give them a bronzed appearance. Tree growth and size of crop are reduced.

Scales

The San Jose scale has caused considerable damage to fruit trees. The scale is about the diameter of a pin head. This flat circular scale is ashy brown, with a raised center.

Apple tree borer

This is a large beetle with two white lines along its back. The larva, a white grub an inch long with a brown head, bores into the trunk of the tree at or just below the ground line.

Other insects

Apple red bug, apple leaf hopper, green fruit worm, casebearer, fall webworm, Japanese beetle, and cankerworm sometimes cause trouble, but are of minor importance.

Diseases

Apple scab

This is the most serious disease of apples in many areas. However, if any disease develops it is serious. The apple scab, besides damaging the current apple crop, weakens the tree and reduces future crops. The fungus overwinters on old leaves and infects the leaves the next spring.

Fire blight

A bacterial disease that attacks apple and pear trees. It is transmitted by bees, insects, aphids and pruning tools. It usually attacks blossoms first and then shoots. The shoots turn brown and remain on the tree. During the dormant season, remove all infected parts 3 to 4 inches below the obvious infection. Disinfect the tools and the wounds.

Apple rust

This disease infects the fruit and sometimes the foliage. The fungus causing the rust spends part of its life on the red cedar tree. Eradicate any red cedar growing next to the orchard.

Black rot

This is a fungus disease also known as *blossom end rot* and on leaves as *leaf spot*. Rhode Island Greening and Baldwin varieties are very susceptible to this disease.

Powdery mildew
    This disease is normally caused by high-humidity conditions. It stunts growth and causes problems in the nursery.

Varieties

    Selecting the variety to plant is a choice that you must make yourself. Apple varieties have originated as the result of a carefully designed breeding program or a chance sport. Careful selection and breeding has resulted in the development of new varieties for areas previously not suited for growing apples. The Anna and Ein Shemer developed in Israel and Tropical Beauty developed in South Africa are good examples of "low chilling" varieties that have extended the southern limits of apple growing. Another "low chilling" variety available for the deep south is Mollie's Delicious. Check with local growers for suggestions on varieties that produce best. You should widen your choices to the extent possible to take advantage of varieties that ripen at different times. Listed are some of the varieties that have stood the test of time. They are listed in their order of ripening.

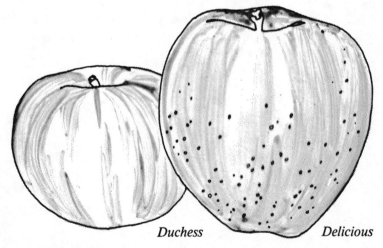

Duchess   *Delicious*

Summer varieties
    1. **Quinte.** Red, superior quality for early season. They are hardy, but subject to scab. Origin or seedling Melba x Crimson Beauty.
    2. **Yellow Transparent.** Yellow. Hardy, but a biennial bearer.

3. **Lodi.** Yellow. Hardy tree and an annual bearer.

4. **Melba.** Red, good quality, tree vigorous, hardy, early bearer. Tends to be biennial. McIntosh seedling.

5. **Duchess.** Red striped, good cooking apple. Very hardy, heavy biennial bearer.

6. **Early McIntosh.** Red, fair quality, requires thinning. Tree vigorous and hardy.

Early fall varieties

1. **Joyce.** Striped, large, good quality, hardy and early bearer.

2. **Gravensteen.** Red, sports are highly colored. Good size and quality. Tree is vigorous and an annual bearer.

3. **Wealthy.** Red, good cooking apple; tree hardy, early biennial bearer.

4. **Lobo.** Red, large, good quality; tree hardy, strong and an annual bearer.

Late fall varieties

1. **McIntosh.** Red, excellent appearance and quality. Good keeper, hardy, vigorous, annual bearer. Subject to scab and fruit dropping.

2. **Cortland.** Red blush. Firm white flesh of good quality.

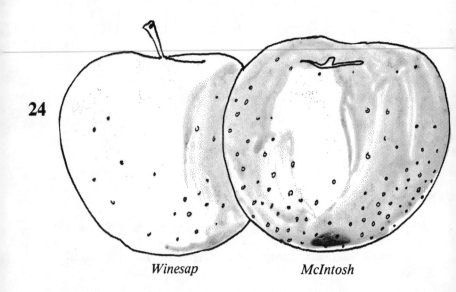

Winesap   *McIntosh*

3. **Ben Davis.** Red, hardy, good keeper.

4. **Spartan.** Red, good color, good quality. Stays on the tree good and is more free from scab than McIntosh.

5. **Delicious.** Red striped, some solid red sports. Conical shape with five points at the end. Fine eating apple. Tree is upright and has narrow crotch angles. Needs good deep soil.

6. **Grimes.** Yellow, good quality, subacid. Better suited to southern apple areas.

7. **Jonathan.** Red, medium-sized, good quality. Tree is medium size, good cropper. Not adapted to northern areas.

8. **Rhode Island Greening.** Green. Good cooking apple, stores well. Spreading tree, moderately hardy.

9. **Stayman.** Red, good color, fair quality. Tree moderately vigorous, suited to warm areas.

10. **Golden delicious.** Yellow, same form as delicious. Very good quality. Tree moderately hardy; not suited to northern areas.

11. **York.** Red, lopsided. Good quality, good keeper. Tree likes rich soil and warm climate.

12. **Winesap.** Red. Good quality, smallish, tart, good keeper, good cooking apple. Tree medium-sized, vigorous in southern area.

13. **Rome.** Red or yellowish-red. Firm, fair quality, good keeper. Tree medium-sized and moderately vigorous. Not adapted to northern areas.

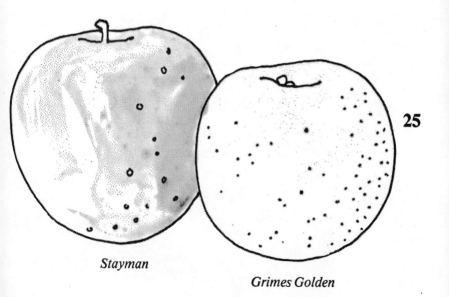

Stayman

Grimes Golden

The Peach

The fruit of the peach is a drupe. It develops entirely from a superior ovary and consists of the outer skin, the middle of the ovary wall that becomes the edible portion, and the inner portion that is hard and becomes the seed. Botanically the peach is of the family *Prunus persica*.

Peaches are produced commercially in about two-thirds of the states of the United States. California is responsible for approximately 50% of the total U.S. production with South Carolina and

Georgia ranking next in line. In the past 10 years northern Florida has become a major growing center. The United States produces about 80% of the peaches worldwide.

In a mature orchard production may average 3 to 5 bushels of peaches per tree; however, because of frost damage, yields vary from year to year. Commercial production may often be a more hazardous enterprise than apple growing because of greater susceptibility to damage from spring frost and low temperatures. The area with the most regular production is California.

Planning and Preparation

Varieties

When planning the peach orchard, consider planting several varieties, starting with early ripening peaches and progressing through a series of ripening periods on into the very late ripening varieties. This will allow you to utilize your labor to best advantage and not have to rely on outside help so much during harvesting season. It also spreads your marketing over a longer period of time, which is very helpful if you're planning roadside-type marketing.

Site location

Even though you're probably limited in your site selection, a slight slope or rolling terrain allows for better air drainage and lessens frost damage. Cold air drains away from high land into lower levels. A variation in elevation of 20 to 30 feet would afford adequate air drainage and may also give frost protection. In general, a northeastern exposure is desirable because it may prevent too early bloom and reduce the possibility of winter injury.

Soil

A deep, well-drained soil that permits extensive root penetration develops trees that live a long time, produce many peaches, and withstand drought, excessive rain, and low winter temperatures.

27

The peach tree has an extensive root system for its size. Roots of a 5-year-old tree may penetrate 10 feet in some soils, even though 90% of the small feeder roots will be in the top 18 inches of soil. The deep root may be of great value during drought and for anchorage during wind storms. The roots will spread farther out than the spread of the branches.

If you plant your peach tree in soil with a high water table or a hard impervious soil layer, trees may be blown over by the wind.

During dry periods, trees will not make normal growth and will produce low yields or fruit of poor size and quality.

Planting

Preparing to plant

The best time to plant the trees is in very early spring, 3 to 4 weeks before the leaf buds break. If trees are transplanted in late spring, the buds force the leaves to bloom too quickly. Sometimes the new root system cannot absorb enough moisture and nutrients for growth and the trees may be killed by spring or summer growth.

Late fall planting is satisfactory in the south; however, fall-planted trees should be watered and cared for during the winter as they may dry out considerably. Late fall planting is not generally wise in the northern regions. In all regions, plant the trees during the dormant period of the trees.

Two types of nursery peach trees are available: the 1-year-old and the June budded. The 1-year-old tree is preferred by most growers; however, in the south the June budded peach tree gives good results and is usually available at a cheaper price.

When you receive trees from the nursery, plant them immediately. Do not allow the roots to dry out. If you cannot plant the trees because of the soil or weather conditions, they should be "heeled-in" to protect them until they can be planted. Make every effort to order the trees so that they will arrive at the proper time for planting. Many trees arrive from the nursery so weakened from being dried out that they get a very poor start or fail to live altogether.

Planting the trees

If you are planting peach trees for commercial production, space them 20 feet x 25 feet at planting time. This will allow space for equipment to work around the trees without damaging them. It will require 70 trees to plant one acre at this spacing.

28

1. Before you plant the peach trees, prune off any broken or diseased roots. Prevent the roots from drying out.
2. Hand-dig holes large enough in width and depth to accommodate the tree roots without crowding them.
3. Distribute the roots in the hole in their natural positions. This will anchor the tree properly at planting time and in the future.
4. Set the tree 1 to 2 inches deeper than it grew in the nursery with the union bud showing just above the ground.

5. Use the top soil as backfill around the roots. Top soil contains more organic matter and mineral nutrients than subsoil.
6. Press the soil firmly around the roots.
7. Use enough water to insure that all air pockets have been eliminated.

29

Peach Tree

Pruning and Thinning

The trees in a peach orchard require pruning for four reasons: 1) to train the tree to a strong framework; 2) to shape the tree within a reasonable size for harvesting; 3) to thin the crops to achieve good size of fruit and yield; 4) to maintain adequate shoot growth. Peach trees need to be pruned every year.

Pruning at planting time

Prune the peach trees immediately after, rather than before, planting. The pruning should reduce the top to balance the loss of roots and the shock of transplanting and should promote the selection of a suitable framework.

Most peach trees are grown close together for a year in the nursery and have few, if any, laterals which are desirable for framework branches. To develop laterals, use the following procedure.

1. Cut back the strongest laterals to 1 to 2 bud stubs (almost a whip). Do not select leading branches at this time.
2. During the first growing season, remove suckers originating below the point of nursery budding and watersprouts on the trunk below the desired height or head level.
3. In the deep south, cut back the tree to a single stem 24 inches high.

PEACH BEFORE PRUNING

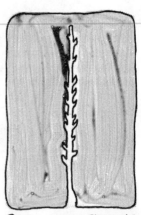

PEACH AFTER PRUNING

4. If laterals have formed, cut the lower ones off flush with the stem, but allow a 1 to 2 inch stub to remain on the upper ones to insure leaving buds for new shoot development.
5. After the tree sprouts in the spring, select three evenly spaced vigorous shoots to be the main scaffolding.
6. Remove or cut back other shoots and remove watersprouts and suckers.
7. Keep the tree growing low for easy picking in later years.
8. Continue this procedure for the second and third years.

Pruning a year-old tree
1. After the peach trees have grown for a year in the orchard, in late winter select 3 strong, well-placed, wide-angled, outward-growing laterals for scaffold branches and remove all others.
2. If two branches of equal size tend to divide the tree and form a "Y" at the trunk, remove one of them.
3. Head-back branches lightly to an outward growing lateral.
4. Keep the tree symmetrical with an aim to developing a good open tree. The framework for most trees after two years in the orchard should consist of three main scaffolds plus secondary branches.
5. After that, the tree should receive only light to moderate pruning, mostly thinning out to keep the center open and fruiting branches well spaced.

Pruning a mature tree
After the peach orchard has matured, prune the trees more heavily than any other fruit trees. The peach tree responds to proper pruning and declines with neglect more than any other fruit tree.

The objectives in pruning mature peach trees are to promote shoots of the right production length and to keep the tree open. The terminal growth of 8 to 18 inches on the outer branches carry blossoms from end to end and make the maximum yield. The fruit is borne laterally on wood of the past year's growth. Long shoots of over 24 inches are not very fruitful and short 3 to 4 inch shoots have little fruit on them. In mature trees most of the fruit will be in the top 1/3 to 1/2 of the tree. The average mature peach tree will produce as many as 25,000 buds. If 10% survive, there is plenty to set a good crop of fruit.

Small orchards can best be pruned in the early spring before growth starts. This leaves the wounds open for a shorter period of time before the callus begins to heal over. Prune the older trees first, finishing with the younger trees.

Limbs and branches pruned from the trees should be removed from the orchard and burned. Do not burn brush in or near the orchard. Trees and branches may be seriously damaged by a comparatively small fire.

Thinning a bearing tree

You should practice thinning the peaches from the tree in order to improve the size, grade and finish of the fruit. It reduces

PEACH BEFORE PRUNING

PEACH AFTER PRUNING

limb breakage and maintains tree vigor. The actual cost of labor for thinning will be offset by improved fruit and less labor at harvest time.

There are not firm set times when thinning is best done; however, a good rule of thumb is to thin shortly after the first fruit drop or when the fruit size is from marble to walnut size. Thin the fruit to a fixed spacing such as 6 to 8 inches along the twig. When thinning, consider leaf area, tree vigor and bearing capacity.

If you intend to market your peaches for table consumption, remember that people prefer a large, sweet, juicy peach. Because No. 2 peaches are of less value, thin the fruit enough so that your peaches will reach No. 1 size.

The leaf area is very important in thinning. Peaches increase in size with greater leaf areas. The sugar content of peaches has also been found to increase as the leaf area increases. The number of leaves per fruit to be left after thinning varies with the variety and tree vigor. Usually, however, 30 to 40 leaves per fruit are desirable.

Peach trees are not, like some apple trees, biennial bearers. Even after an excessive crop, peach trees can produce a crop the next year. Thinning year after year will help the tree avoid exhaustion as a result of the overproduction of pits, the development of which draws heavily on the tree's mineral supply.

Use the hand method to thin the fruit. Rub off the surplus fruit by hand to the desired spacing and break up clusters. If there are difficult places to reach or if time is short, a 1½-inch diameter pole with a rubber hose 15 to 18 inches long can be used to strike into the clusters along the branches toward the outside of the tree or limb. Do not knock off any more leaves than necessary when thinning the fruit.

Soil Management

The soil management system used for peach orchards will depend on the soil, the slope and water availability. The most conventional soil management system is cultivation with cover crops and an annual application of fertilizers. Mulching around the trees with hay, corn cobs, straw and such materials fits well into this program. This system is effective because it retards runoff and leaching of minerals, helps maintain or increase the level of organic matter in the soil, aids in water penetration, checks fall growth and thereby encourages maturing of the tree tissue, and helps stabilize the soil temperature.

Sod system

The best sites for peach orchards are often on elevated land with steep slopes to reduce the hazard from spring frost. Therefore, a sod system may be desirable to reduce erosion and water runoff. Sod systems require substantial amounts of water and fertilizer to obtain good growth and yields. Young trees must be fertilized and watered to achieve good growth rates. Herbicides can be used to hold down growth of grass around the trees themselves. When using herbicides, use only those which have been cleared for young and/or bearing peach trees, and follow the manufacturer's directions carefully.

Cover crop

Trash farming, where the residue of the cover crop is left on the surface, is a system that works well in some orchards. The litter, trash, and roughness of the soil surface reduce soil erosion. The stubble mulch also prepares the soil so that it will receive more rainfall, and there will be much less run-off.

Cultivation

On level soils that tend to be droughty, cultivation prevents competition for moisture by other vegetation. If you don't have an irrigation system, cultivate mature trees in spring and early summer. If you have young trees, you may continue to cultivate them slightly later.

You may want to practice intensive culture and plant early maturing vegetables between the rows of young trees. Do not work the soil more than 3 to 4 inches deep beneath the trees.

Irrigation

An irrigation system in the peach orchard is one of the best insurances you can have. Even in high rainfall areas, 2 or 3 weeks of dry, hot weather during pit hardening and final swell period will adversely affect fruit size. A deficiency of moisture during the growing season may result in less terminal growth and reduce winter hardiness. Sprinkler irrigation systems can be used to help prevent frost damage. Sprinkling can also reduce temperatures on abnormally warm early spring days, thereby holding back budding trees from early blooming. This will prevent the trees from being damaged by later frost.

In watering peach trees, use enough water to penetrate the soil to the roots. A light wetting of the top few inches is a waste of time. An excessive amount of water leaches the nutrients out of the soil and raises the water table, restricting the root zone for the tree. If the soil is shallow, you will need less water but will need to irrigate more often.

Fertilizing

The fertilizer program needs to be part of the overall orchard management and needs to be balanced with the soil management and pruning programs. It is usually necessary to fertilize peach trees annually. The amount and kind of fertilizer to use will depend on the soil and leaf analyses, which have become increasingly efficient and available to growers. Your county agent can arrange these services for you.

Nitrogen

Nitrogen stimulates growth and the peach is a nitrogen-demanding tree. Trees well supplied with nitrogen have dark green leaves, long thick shoots, and large fleshy fruit. However, under conditions of high nitrogen supply, the maturity may be delayed with the fruit ripening unevenly. In that case, you may need to make 3 or 4 pickings. Excess nitrogen may cause poor fruit color, lack of normal sweetness, and lack of peach aroma.

Nitrogen is normally applied in early spring at the general rate of about 1/3 to 1/2 pound per inch of trunk diameter near the base, using 20% nitrogen fertilizer. Another guide is to supply about 0.3 pounds of nitrogen of soda for each year of the tree's age, up to a maximum of 4 to 5 pounds per mature tree. Apply ammonium nitrate at about half that rate. Most nitrogen fertilizer is broadcast on the soil, generally in a two foot band under the outer edge or perimeter of the tree where the feeder roots are most numerous. It is not necessary to work nitrogen fertilizer into the soil as it will soon penetrate the root zone.

Phosphorus

35

The peach tree is not a heavy feeder of phosphorous. The need is probably greater for the cover crops or sod than the trees themselves. Symptoms of phosphorous deficiency in peach trees are indicated by the older leaves becoming mottled with light green areas between dark green veins, progressive defoliation of mottled leaves from base to tip of twigs as the season advances, and purplish pigment development in leaf petioles in cold weather.

Phosphorus should be applied as soil tests indicate the need. In most cases, the application of a complete fertilizer on the cover crop will meet all the tree's requirements for phosphorus.

Potassium

The peach tree requires potassium in almost as large amounts as nitrogen. Potassium aids in formation of carbohydrates, tends to improve quality, and influences the tree's resistance to diseases and cold. Potassium remains in the soil longer than nitrogen and stays available to the trees longer; therefore, application of potassium fertilizers is not required very often. As a general rule, potassium will need to be applied at about half the rate of nitrogen.

Other elements

Boron, zinc, magnesium, manganese and iron may sometimes show up as deficient in peach trees. Leaf analyses will indicate these deficiencies and the proper steps can be taken to correct them.

Winter Injury

Peaches are more subject to winter injury and spring frost than apples and pears because the peach tree blooms earlier. In general, the more advanced the bloom, the greater the injury from a given temperature. The fruit buds of peaches may be killed at -10° to 20°F during the winter months, depending on the duration of the low temperature and whether the cold occurred suddenly or slowly.

Open blooms will generally show damage at 26°F. Following petal fall, the young fruit will be injured at 28°F. When you expect frost conditions, use smudge pots or, if available, a very fine water spray. Growers use sprinkler irrigation systems by extending the risers and installing the fogger-mist type nozzles in early spring. Also, a partial protection against spring frost is a bare hard soil surface in the orchard from early pink to about 10 days after the petals fall. Clear, sunny days often precede nights when frost kill occurs. If the orchard floor is bare, it stores a large amount of heat from the sun and the heat is then radiated into the air at night.

Harvesting

When you decide to pick your peach crop depends upon how you intend to market the crop. If you plan to sell the peaches to local stores, let them become nearly ripe on the trees. For long shipment or for storage before being sold, pick the fruit when it is still firm (mature ripe). Fruit that is to be marketed in roadside stands or sold direct to the consumer (pick your own) should be "tree ripe."

The best index of maturity is the disappearance of the green from the background color of the peach. As peaches approach maturity, the leaf-green color turns lighter. As the peach becomes riper, the green turns a yellow or yellow-orange on yellow-fleshed varieties and turns a cream color on white types. Red color is not a reliable index of maturity. A red cheeked peach may not be sufficiently ripe.

You can test the peach's firmness by placing the peach in the palm of your hand; as you close your hand, you can feel the "give." The local trade taste is probably the best method to be sure that the peaches are at the right degree of ripeness.

Peaches are commonly packed in ring tub-type veneer baskets in half-bushel and bushel sizes. The ring tub-basket pack provides a uniform surface so each fruit receives a part of the pressure. It also shows the fruit well.

Insects

Spray schedules for pests vary in different regions and change frequently. You must obtain a spray schedule recommended for your area and stick with it religiously. Peaches cannot be raised without good insect and disease control.

Plum curculio

The adult is a rough-looking greyish to dark brown snouted beetle with a hump on the middle of each wing cover. The beetle attacks the fruit soon after the petals fall and causes injury both by feeding and by egg laying. The beetle also may introduce brown rot spores in the fruit.

Oriental fruit moth

The larvae of the first hatch attack the tips of growing shoots and burrow into them. Terminal leaves wilt, turn brown and die. They usually remain on the tree for several days before falling. Later hatches attack both the shoots and the fruit when they are about 2/3 grown. Wormy fruit results. The larvae are pinkish-white.

Stinkbugs

A sucking bug that attacks the fruit and will cause fruit gummosis.

San Jose scale

Causes the surface of the bark on the tree to become rough and grey in color. Weakens the tree and opens the trunk up to other diseases.

Shot-hole borer

Trees weakened by San Jose scale are often victims of the shot-hole borer, which causes small spots of gummy exudate to occur on twigs, branches, and sometimes the trunk.

Japanese beetle

The adults are about 1/2 inch long and have a shiny body. They skeletonize the foliage and eat holes in the ripening fruit.

Mites

They feed by withdrawing the liquid contents of the cells. In large numbers they cause a bronzed or greyish leaf color. They impair the quality and size of the fruit.

JAPANESE BEETLE

PLUM CURCULIO

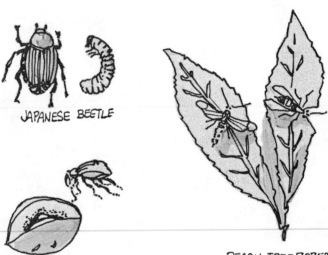

PEACH-TREE BORER

SAN JOSE SCALE

HARLEQUIN BUG
(stinkbug)

Disease

To assure yourself of healthy fruit, you should spray to prevent diseases just as you spray to prevent insect damage.

Peach leaf curl

The leaves become thickened, curled or crinkled, and yellowish. The diseased leaves fall in early summer, thus weakening the tree.

Brown rot

First appears as a small, brown spot. The blemish increases until the whole fruit becomes soft, brown and rotten. Control of the insects that puncture the fruit is also required to control brown rot.

Peach scab

Appears as small, round, olive-black spots on the fruit, usually on the upper part. When the spots run together, the fruit is stunted and deformed.

Peach rust

May cause premature defoliation.

Peach canker

One of the worst pests of peach trees. Canker causes gummy cankers on the limbs and twig blight in the tops of the trees, often followed by heart rot.

Bacterial spot

Sign of the disease is purple, brown, angular spots on the leaves that die out and cause premature defoliation.

Varieties

Many varieties of peaches can be grown in the United States, but some are more adaptable to certain locations than others. Be sure to select varieties that are well adapted to your location. Some varieties require as much as 1200 hours of chilling at a temperature below 45°F to keep trees dormant during the winter. Others, adapted to the Deep South, require only 50 hours of low chilling at a temperature of 45°F.

If you choose a variety that requires more chilling than the average for your area, your trees may bloom late and reduce spring hazard, but they will probably fail to set fruit satisfactorily because of inadequate winter chilling. Varieties with low chilling requirements that are planted in colder climates bloom too early and fruit is generally lost to spring frost.

The most desirable selection is from varieties that have a chilling requirement slightly higher than the minimum February accumulation of the locality involved. A rest period of this intensity, following normal or colder than normal winters, delays blooming until the frost hazard is reduced. It does not cause serious prolonged dormancy trouble following milder winters. Varieties with slightly higher chilling requirements may succeed if they have strong fruit setting habits.

The local county agent will have good information as to what varieties are best adapted to your locality. Local nurserymen can also supply helpful information in regard to varieties and rootstock that is best adapted to your locality.

Select a series of varieties that will ripen over the longest period possible, both for home use and local marketing. Certain varieties are suitable for all markets; however, some are more desirable for one specific purpose, such as making pickled peaches. The preferred flesh color is yellow. Only a few commercial varieties are now white-fleshed.

Below is a description of the **four main groups** or races of peaches.

1. **South China.** This race has small fruit, white flesh, a sweet honey-like flavor and low acidity. It also has astringent skin, dull fruit color and poor shipping quality. It does have a low chilling requirement and the fruit ripens early. Jewel and Okinawa are examples of this race.

2. **Spanish.** The fruit is small, low in quality. This race is raised occasionally in the Deep South.

3. **Persian.** This race includes varieties that were imported from England and Italy. Persian peaches have high quality and a large amount of red color. The Early Crawford and Late Crawford are examples of this race.

40

4. **North China.** This is a race that was one of the parents of a number of white-fleshed varieties, such as Belle of Georgia and Greensboro. Its most famous off-spring is the Elberta peach, which has been the standard for peach growers for years; however, Elberta is now losing out to other varieties such as Suncrest, Redhaven and Redskin.

Most varieties trace back to North China race or the Persian race or crosses between the two. Some of the more popular varieties and their characteristics are listed in order of their ripening, based on the time of Elberta's ripening season.

Very early varieties (50 to 60 days before Elberta)

1. **Earlyvee.** Yellow, highly colored, fair quality, semi-freestone. Good for tree-ripened fruit sales. Tree comes into bearing early. Chilling requirements medium.

2. **Candor.** Bright red blush, rich yellow color, semi-freestone. Developed in North Carolina. Approximately 850 chilling hours required.

3. **Earlired.** Bright red color, good size, needs thinning. Developed in Maryland.

4. **Maygold.** Yellow, small- to medium-sized fruit. Not adapted to the north. Low chilling requirements of 650 hours.

Early varieties (30-40 days before Elberta)

1. **Jerseyland.** Red color, medium-sized fruit, freestone, fairly firm when ripe. Developed in New Jersey. Approximately 800 chilling hours required.

2. **Coronet.** Red blush, medium-sized, freestone. Developed in Georgia.

3. **Sunhaven.** Medium-sized, round, uniform. Developed in Michigan. Chilling requirement approximately 900 hours.

4. **Sentinel.** Red blush over yellow background color. Medium-sized, fairly firm. Developed in Georgia. Chilling requirement 800 hours.

5. **Other varieties.** Royalvee, Garnet Beauty, Harbelle, Dixiegen, Redcap, Marigold, and Prairie Dawn.

Midseason varieties (7-25 days before Elberta)

1. **Redhaven.** Solid red skin color. Will color before ripening. A superior variety for the East and Midwest. Has been very popular in California, but is declining because it is not as good a long distance shipper as some other varieties. Chilling requirement 850 hours.

2. **Golden Jubilee.** Elberta-type fruit, soft, bruises easily, freestone. Was widely grown in South Carolina, but has lost out to other varieties. Chilling requirement 850 hours.

3. **Harmony**. Better than average quality, high producer, medium-sized, firm. Very winter hardy, excellent variety for cold climates. Chilling requirement 1000 hours or more.

4. **Suncrest**. Excellent producer of fresh fruit. A leading producer in California. Developed by the U.S. Department of Agriculture.

5. **Other varieties**. Envoy, Ranger, Loring, Veteran, Velvet, Southland, Sunhigh, Hiley (white), Fairhaven, Keystone, Washington, Redglobe, Fireball, July Elberta, Early Elberta, Triogen, Halehaven, J.H. Hale, Belle of Georgia (white), and Madison.

Elberta season varieties

1. **Elberta**. At one time Elberta was extensively planted. It has good size, firmness, and is adapted to a wide range of soils. Newer, improved varieties have largely replaced the Elberta. Chillings hours 850.

2. **Blake**. Red colored, freestone, large, firm, roundish. Tree not too hardy in the north.

42

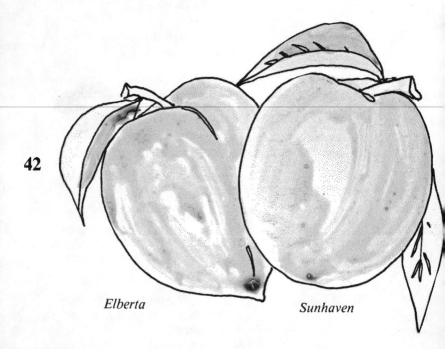

Elberta   *Sunhaven*

3. **Redskin.** Red color, medium-sized fruit, freestone. Better quality and color than Elberta. Developed in Maryland. Chilling requirement 750 hours.

4. **Other varieties.** Fay Elberta, Dixieland, Olinda, Jefferson and Jerseyqueen. Varieties a few days later than Elberta include Rio Oso Gem, Afterglow, Suncling, and the California Clingstones.

Some varieties with low chilling requirements have been developed for the Deep South and Gulf Coast area. Most of these varieties have only fair quality and should be tree ripened. These varieties include Junegold, Early Amber, Rio Grande, Sam Houston, Okinawa, White Knight, Floridawon, Floridabelle, and the one with the lowest chilling requirement, Ceylon, that requires only 50 to 100 chilling hours.

The Nectarine

Botanically, the nectarine *(Prunus persica)*, like the peach, is a drupe fruit. It is a seed sport of peach. Genetically, the nectarine character is due to a single recessive gene in its parent, the peach.

Horticulturally, the peach and nectarine trees differ in no essential respect from each other in appearance, growth responses, bearing habits, or general characteristics. The nectarine has greater aroma and a more distinct flavor and is without the fuzz that is characteristic of the peach. Consider planting a variety or two in your peach orchard, especially if you plan to do roadside marketing.

Orchard management should be the same for nectarines as it is for peaches. The curculio and brown rot are probably even more of a menace to nectarines than to peaches; therefore, a good pest control program is a must.

Varieties

Some varieties of nectarines will grow satisfactorily in any area where peaches are grown. Commercial production has been almost wholly in California. Great strides have been made in breeding improved varieties in the West; therefore, much better varieties are available there. The most popular varieties consist of Early Sun, Sun Grand, Merrill Sunrise, Grand River and Merrill Princess. All of these are patented. Other available varieties are Burbank's Flaming Gold, Stanwych and Goldmine.

The recent development of new low chilling varieties has increased nectarine production in the East. Sunred and Sungold are two such varieties. The former matures in the week of May 10th and the latter in the week of June 10th. These are excellent for the early market in the East.

Some of the nectarines developed in the East are Nectarose (white fleshed), Nectaheart (white), Nectacrest (white), Nectared (yellow), Garden State (yellow), Nectalate (white), Cavalier (yellow), Pocahontas (yellow), Cherokee (yellow), Red Chief (white), Hunter (yellow), Morton (white), Early Flame, Earliblaze, Red Gold, Sun Glo, Sun Red, and Sungold (yellow).

Because the nectarines are fuzzless and a softer fruit, they must be handled even more carefully than peaches.

The Pear

Botanically, the pear is very closely related to the apple. Like the apple, the pear fruit is classed as a pome. Each of the fine leathery carpels contains 2 seeds. The receptacle and ovary wall become fleshy to constitute the edible portions of the fruit.

Although pears are produced commercially almost entirely in the area west of the Rocky Mountains, they are grown all over the United States. In the South they are grown below the southern limits of apples. Varieties such as Orient, Kieffer, Pineapple, Baldwin and Hood have low enough chilling requirements to succeed well as far south as northern Florida, but the quality of the fruit is not as good as that produced in California.

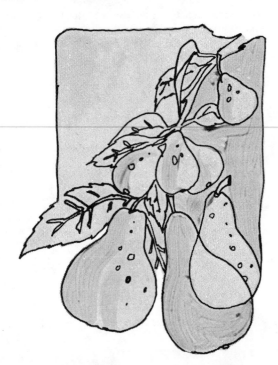

Planning and Preparation

Precipitation

The pear tree should receive at least 35 inches of rainfall evenly distributed during the growing season. If this amount is not normally available, provisions should be made for irrigation.

Temperature

Pear trees that are fully dormant can withstand low temperatures of about −20°F. The wood and buds of pears seem somewhat more subject to injury from low temperatures than those of apples, but they are more resistant to low temperatures than peach trees. In general, pear growing is hazardous where temperatures may be lower than −15 to −20°F.

Site location

Freedom from spring frost is important in pear orchards; hence, the slopes of rolling land are preferable to obtain good air drainage. Pears normally bloom several days before apples, and the blossoms are about as easily damaged by frost.

Soil

Pears grow in a wide range of soils, but they grow best in deep fertile loams with a well-drained subsoil. There should be at least 4 feet of soil in which the roots can penetrate freely. A deeper soil will hold more moisture and a greater reserve of nutrients.

Planting

Preparing to plant

Prepare the land for planting a pear orchard by cultivating it for a year or two. Turning under a green manure crop or raising legumes would be helpful. If the site is on very much of a slope, contour or terrace the land.

Early spring is the ideal time to plant pear trees. If you cannot plant trees when they are received from the nursery, they should be "heeled in" by laying them in a trench and covering the roots and about a foot of the trunk with moist soil. Keep moist until planting. Do not let the roots dry out. Keep moist and protected when planting.

Planting the trees

1. Stake tree locations in a triangle or square 25 feet x 25 feet.
2. Dig the holes deep enough to set the trees one or two inches deeper than they were growing in the nursery.
3. Remove long and damaged roots.

4. Spread the roots out in the hole without crowding them. Use a planting board to keep the trees in line while planting.
5. Use top soil to backfill the hole.
6. Add enough water to eliminate any air pockets around the roots.

Pruning

Pruning at planting time

If the nursery tree is an unbranched whip, cut it off to a height of 40 to 48 inches.

Pruning a year-old tree

Select 4 to 5 vigorous branches, 6 to 12 inches apart, well distributed along the trunk for the main framework. Remove the other limbs. Make the central branch dominate. Such a distribution of branches gives a stronger tree and reduces the chances of blight.

Pruning a bearing tree

After a tree starts bearing, the purpose of pruning is to maintain the spurs and fruiting wood in good condition. Pruning practices for bearing trees should be correlated with soil management and other cultural practices. Careful study of variety characteristics and the influence of local conditions and treatments of them is necessary in evolving the best pruning system.

Soil Management

The soil management for pear orchards should vary with the locations, but you should avoid any practices that promote too succulent growth. This will help you control fire blight, the pear's most destructive disease.

Cover crops

Most pear orchard management systems are based on permanent covers, such as grasses and legumes, which protect the soil. They reduce leaching of water-soluble nutrients from the soil, minimize the cost of cultivation, and supply organic material for the soil.

Seed the area between the trees, preferably before the trees reach full bearing age. Allow the crop to grow throughout the season and mat down to form a dense soil cover during late summer.

In spring disk the ground to incorporate the vegetation. This system requires more moisture, and the heavy vegetation tends to harbor insects.

Mulching

Pear trees also thrive when mulched. Mulching generally consists of applying straw, hay or other such materials beneath the tree from near the trunk out to the drip line of the branches. This material should be maintained deep enough to completely smother vegetation. Many pear growers have found mulching increases the

Pear Tree

yield of improved quality fruit, saves on fertilizer costs, produces better tree growth, and has a beneficial effect on the soil. Follow good mouse control program when you use mulch.

Fertilizing

The best guide to fertilizer requirements of pear trees is the appearance and condition of the trees themselves. Soil tests can give an indication of minerals that are lacking, but they do not indicate if the tree is making proper use of minerals in the soil. Tissue tests of the leaves are a better indicator in the pear tree.

Nitrogen

Fertilizing pear trees with nitrogen requires close attention. Some nitrogen is usually needed to obtain good production and good quality; however, if the tree produces excessive succulent growth, it is much more likely to contact fire blight. As an average for bearing pear trees, an annual program of applying 6-8 pounds of 10-10-10 or equal fertilizer should do the job. If any trace mineral deficiencies show, they should be corrected.

Pollination

All pear varieties are commercially self-unfruitful, but some inconsistency exists. Bartlett, for example, is considered self-fruitful in some areas such as the Sacramento Valley in California. Cross-pollination will improve fruit set in those locations. Most varieties can satisfactorily pollinate others if the bloom period has sufficient overlap. Some early bloomers like Kieffer, Howell and Duchess may not be good pollinizers for later bloomers such as Winter Nelis and Wilder. Avoid pollinizers that are particularly susceptible to fire blight.

Honeybees are the chief agents of cross-pollination even though pear blossoms have very little nectar and are not very attractive to honeybees. The wind plays very little part in pollination because pear pollen is very heavy.

Harvesting

Pears should be picked when fully mature but still hard and green. If left on the tree until fully ripe, pears break down and turn brown next to the core. If picked too early before they mature, they will not keep or develop their flavor. Mature pears will ripen in 5 to 7 days after being picked if held at room temperature.

Probably the best indication of maturity is how the pear separates from the spur. At optimum maturity for picking, they usually can be separated from the spur by a slight twisting pull. Generally, if a large percentage of spurs come off with the pear, they are not ready to be picked. Begin picking as soon as sound pears start dropping from the tree.

Most varieties of pears can be stored at low temperatures for 2 to 3 months. A few varieties can be stored for as long as 5 to 6 months. However, you probably won't have the necessary cold storage equipment for such long term storage. Pears can be stored without refrigeration for a period of 2 or 3 weeks if they are kept in a cool, dark place.

Insects

A local spray control schedule should be obtained and followed to control insects and diseases. Careful timing and thoroughness is required to obtain the best results from chemical pesticides and fungicides. Most of the insects that attack apple trees will also damage pear trees. In addition, the following need to be controlled.

Pear psylla

The adult and the nymphs suck juice from the leaves, fruit stem and young shoots.

Pear thrip

These minute brown and grey insects injure the open blossoms and give the leaves a blistered look.

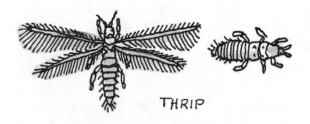

THRIP

Pear slug

The adult is a black and yellow sawfly. The slug-like larva is greenish black and attacks the young trees. Most insecticides are effective against them.

Blister mites

This insect injures the pear leaves, generally in orchards that are not properly managed.

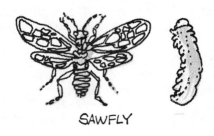

SAWFLY

Diseases

The most destructive disease of pears is caused by the bacterium *amylovora,* commonly called fire blight. It usually appears first as a blossom blight and then spreads to the shoots. The bacteria may enter the trunk and main limbs causing cankers. You can control the disease by removing infected areas. You can prevent the disease by removing all suckers and water sprouts from the tree and employing cultural practices that oppose too vigorous wood growth. All tools used in pruning and cutting should be disinfected before being used on each tree.

52

Scab

This fungus disease appears as dark, moldy patches on both the fruit and leaves. It tends to be worse in areas of high humidity. Sulfur or Captan gives good control.

Black end

This disease makes the fruit hard and stringy. The blossom end turns black as the fruit reaches maturity. The trouble is caused by propagating from Oriental rootstock.

Pear decline

This disease is prevalent in the western United States. It can develop at any time in the life of the tree. The domestic Bartlett seedlings are highly resistant.

Varieties

Choose pear varieties developed for your locality and tested and recommended by your state agricultural experiment station. Provide cross-pollination by planting two or more varieties of pears. Plant only varieties resistant to fire blight if you are located east of the Rocky Mountains.

Pear varieties vary greatly in size, form, quality and disease resistance. Also, considerable variation may occur in the same varieties between areas. Some of the more common varieties are as follows:

1. **Anjou.** Large, good quality, store and ship well. Good pollinizer. Best adapted to West Coast areas.

2. **Bartlett.** This variety produces 75% of the pears produced in the United States. Most of these pears are grown in the three western states. Bartlett does not resist fire blight and should not be

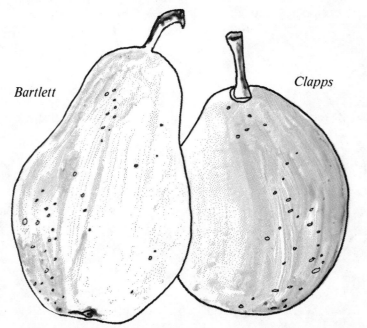

Bartlett

Clapps

planted east of the Rocky Mountains, except around the Great Lakes area where it is cool in the spring. Bartlett fruit is of high quality for desserts, canning and drying.

3. **Bosc.** Large, bell shaped, russet-colored fruit. High quality for desserts and canning. Not recommended for most eastern locations.

4. **Clapp.** Large, attractive, well-colored, very good quality, early.

5. **Giffard.** An early pear of good quality. Green with red dots and red marbling.

6. **Howell.** A large yellow pear of good quality. Stores and handles well.

7. **Kieffer.** Medium-sized, a preserving pear, poor dessert quality. Tree is very productive and has wide adaptability, is hardy, and disease resistant.

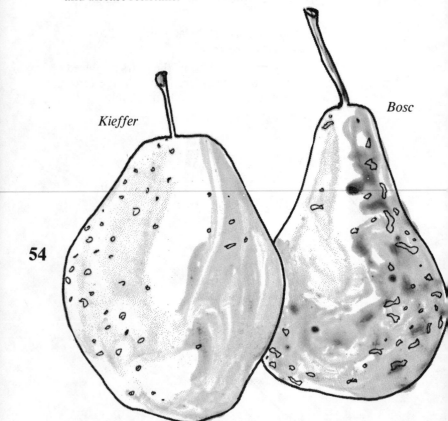

Kieffer

Bosc

54

8. **Magness.** A high quality dessert type adapted to the eastern United States.

9. **Moonglow.** A high quality dessert and canning type for east of the Rocky Mountains.

10. **Seckel.** Small, sweet, high quality. Tree is vigorous, hardy and productive. Succeeds best on dwarfing roots. Fire blight resistant.

11. **Waite.** Fair quality. Good for cooking or canning. Adapted to the east.

12. **Winter Nelis.** Small, attractive, high quality, keeps well. Tree difficult to prune.

Other varieties

Orient, Pineapple, Baldwin and Garber are pears that are showing good results when planted in the deep South. The quality is only fair for dessert, but they will cook and can very well.

Seckel   *Anjou*

The Plum

The plum, like the peach, is a drupe fruit. Because of their wide variety, plums can be grown in most parts of the United States. However, 90% of the total commercial crop is grown in California, Michigan, Oregon, Washington and Idaho.

The large-fruited European-type plum is the most important species. It is botanically known as *Prunus domestica.* In this group are the Prunes, Green Gages, Yellow Eggs, Lombards, and the Blue Imperatricea. All prunes are plums, but not all plums are prunes.

Japanese plums are the next in importance to the large-fruited plum. These are the varieties that are used mostly for eating fresh. The trees are very productive, but they bloom early and are subject to spring frost damage.

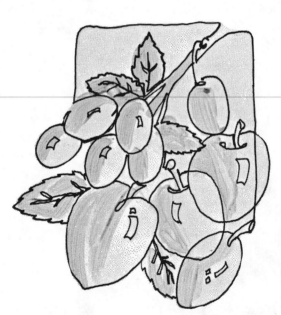

A large group of native plums in the United States can be found in the Deep South, the arid Southwest, the beach along the coast, and the mountain areas. The hardy types have been used in cross-breeding work to produce varieties that are cold hardy or have low chilling requirements and to improve their jelly and jam making quality.

Planning and Preparation

Plum trees should be planted in early spring to avoid winter injury, although fall planting can be done in areas where the winters are mild. Two-year-old trees are usually best for the European type, but 1-year-old whips are suitable for the Japanese types.

Planting

Preparing to plant

Plow and work the soil well before planting. Raise a cultivated crop or two on the area before planting it to plums.

Planting the trees

The best planting distance will vary with the varieties, but a good standard distance is a square or triangle spacing of 20 feet x 20 feet. Planting closer will not leave sufficient room to get equipment around the trees.

1. Dig the holes by hand or with a large tractor-mounted auger.
2. Trim all broken roots before setting.
3. Set the tree slightly deeper than it was growing in the nursery and spread the roots out in the hole.
4. Tamp the soil firmly around the roots.
5. Use water if necessary to have good moist soil next to the roots. Be sure that air pockets are not left around the roots.
6. Use good top soil to backfill the hole since the top soil will have more minerals.
7. Do not put fertilizer in the hole at planting time.

Pruning and Thinning

Pruning at planting time

The plum tree is pruned less than any other fruit tree. Pruning at planting time should consist simply of heading-back to the desired height. If you plan to use existing branches of 2-year-old trees as scaffold branches, select and retain 3 to 5 of them. Head-back primary scaffold branches to 16 to 20 inches in length. The lowest framework branch can be left 24 to 36 inches from the ground. Do not leave too many primary scaffold branches or the head will become very dense.

Pruning a mature tree

Most plum trees will form a good top even though little or no pruning is done. Avoid extreme heading-back, since it is likely to result in long upright growth and a dense top. Prune lightly, mostly in a corrective way and by thinning cuts. Thin the center lightly to admit sunshine, to facilitate spraying and easier harvesting.

The Japanese plum is a prolific bearer. Since large fruits are the most valuable, prune these trees more heavily to reduce the crop and promote sufficient new wood growth.

Certain varieties, such as Burbank, are rather low spreading and should be pruned to divert the growth into more upright branches. The varieties with narrow, upright growth should be pruned through thinning-out cuts to outward-growing branches to develop a more spreading tree.

Thinning a bearing tree

Thinning the plums is not a big problem, because most varieties have enough fruit drop during the growing season. You will need to thin a few of the heavy-bearing Japanese varieties so that the fruit can develop to normal size. Chemical thinning with dinitro 318 at the rate of 1/2 pint per 100 gallons of water will give good results; however, you will probably get better overall results by hand thinning.

Soil Management

The plum does not seem hard to please in soil requirements as long as water drainage is good. A little slope that provides both water and air drainage is better than a dead level area or a pocket. Such a slope may retard blooming and avoid early frost injury.

Soil management for the plum orchard should be a combination of cultivation and cover crops, with mulch directly under the trees. This system helps to hold soil in place and reduces loss of minerals from the soil. Clean cultivation without cover crops sooner or later exhausts the soil of humus.

Fertilizing

You can tell if your plum trees need fertilizer by the condition of the cover crop. If the cover crop is making satisfactory growth, chances are that little if any fertilizer is needed. The best time to apply the fertilizer is just before or at the time of planting the cover crop.

Nitrogen

If trees are making poor growth and have pale green leaves, nitrogen is probably deficient. The amount of nitrogen to apply depends upon the size of the tree. Use a small amount at first and increase as needed. A mature tree should not require more than 1 to 2 pounds of ammonium nitrate.

Phosphorus and potassium

Broadcast these elements over the whole area at the rate indicated by the soil test.

Pollination

Pollination is an important consideration in planting a plum orchard, because most varieties are self-fruitful and some are cross-fruitful as well. European varieties and Japanese varieties are generally incompatible. Varieties that bloom early are not reliable pollinators for late blooming varieties. You need to have at least three varieties that bloom at approximately the same period. Keep honeybees in the plum orchard to insure good pollination.

Harvesting

The growing season for most varieties of plums extends into or through the summer months. You must maintain the soil moisture to obtain yields and mature fruit size. If rainfall is likely to be deficient during these months, provide some type of irrigation in the plum orchard.

Because plums ripen unevenly over the tree, you will need to pick 2 or 3 times to harvest good quality fruit. Plums for eating must be tree-ripened. Plums for jams and jellies can be picked at a slightly earlier time.

Processing Prunes

In some areas of the West, prunes are not harvested from the trees, but are allowed to fall to the ground. They are then processed as dried prunes. Almost all of the commercially produced dried prunes are processed on the West Coast; however, dried prunes of acceptable quality can be made from varieties grown in the East. Examples are Italian, Imperial Epineuse, and President.

Drying French prunes for home use

1. Dip French prune fruits into a solution of 1 pound of lye (caustic soda) to 20 gallons water at about 200°F or near the boiling point. If the skins do not crack readily, use 2 to 3 pounds of lye.
2. Immerse for 5 to 15 seconds. Avoid large cracks or peeling fruit.
3. Rinse well by immersing in running water or spraying.

Drying Imperial prunes

1. Treat Imperial prunes to be sun dried in a very mild lye solution, 1/2 pound to 20 gallons of water for 5 seconds. Handle Imperial prunes with care since they tend to slab easily.
2. After the lye dip, run the fruit over a needle board to make the skins more permeable to water.
3. Place the fruit one layer deep on trays for drying.
4. Leave the prunes in the sun for one week or more, until they are at least 3/4 dry.
5. Stack the trays and let the prunes continue to dry slowly. Bring in the trays if it looks like rain.
6. Do not allow the prunes to dry to the point where they rattle when the trays are shaken. The prunes should feel pliable when a handful is squeezed and separate when released.
7. Store.

Disease and Insects

Timely and thorough application of the proper spray materials will control curculio beetle and brown rot, both of which attack plums. Consult the local county agent for a good spray calendar for the area.

Varieties

The large fruited varieties are preferred by customers. The Japanese-type plum is the leader for early markets in the East, but it is produced in smaller volume than the large European type.

A plum orchard in the East or Midwest should include varieties that are attractive and good in quality. For home use and roadside marketing, select a succession of good fruit suitable for all purposes, from the beginning of the season to the end. The season in the East is from August to October.

The prune is the main commercial plum raised on the West Coast and is sold for eating fresh, for drying and for canning. The Green Gage group is also canned commercially.

European varieties

1. **Queenstone.** Fruit blue, medium-sized, freestone, acceptable market quality.

2. **California Blue.** Large, nearly freestone, fair quality, useful as an early blue plum.

3. **Washington.** Large, roundish oval, light yellow. Flesh is greenish-yellow and firm. Freestone and very good quality. Useful for eating fresh and for home and local markets.

4. **French Prune.** An important variety for making dried prunes. Purplish-red, sweet, smaller than Imperial Epineuse.

5. **Imperial Epineuse.** Grows in the West particularly for drying because it demands a premium price. Reddish-purple fruit, greenish-yellow flesh, sweet.

6. **Iroquois.** Blue, firm fruit. Greenish-yellow flesh. Freestone, fair to good quality. Good for canning. Comes into bearing early.

7. **Early Italian.** Used as a fresh plum. Similar to the Italian except it ripens earlier. **61**

8. **Stanley.** Early bearing and a good pollinator for other European types. A leading variety around the Great Lakes region.

9. **Blue Bell.** Larger than Stanley and about one week later. Blue, yellow flesh, freestone, high quality.

10. **Verity.** Fruit larger than Italian. Blue, orange color flesh, freestone. Good for fresh market and processing.

11. **Valor.** Dark purple, larger than Italian, greenish-gold flesh, semi-freestone. Good for fresh fruit.

12. **Reine Claude.** (Green Gage) Matures in late September in the North. Yellowish-green fruit, medium-sized, roundish oval, golden-yellow flesh. Tender, sweet and mild. The standard green gage plum for canning.

13. **Lombard.** Purplish-red. Makes a good canning fruit. Not attractive for fresh fruit.

14. **President.** Blue-black fruit, good size. Flesh firm and of good quality, freestone.

15. **Albion.** Ripens late (about October 1 in the Great Lakes region) and hangs on through several frosts. Large fruit, oval, purplish-black, golden-yellow flesh, firm, juicy, pleasantly flavored, good quality, clingstone.

16. **Others.** Grand Duke, Bluefre, Jefferson, Sugar, Giant, Yellow Egg, Golden Drop, Arch Duke, Monarch, Diamond, Bradshaw, Pond.

Japanese varieties

1. **Early Golden.** Yellow with reddish blush when mature. Tree vigorous and a biennial bearer. Originated in Canada.

2. **Beauty.** Very early. Medium-sized, roundish, medium red, flesh yellow-tinged with red. Very juicy, sweet, fair in quality.

3. **Bruce.** Red, round, firm, fair in quality. Has considerable merit in Texas for marketing in May.

4. **Methley.** Blood-red flesh, mottled grey on red skin. Does fairly well in the South. New Zealand origin.

5. **Laredo.** Dark red skin, amber flesh, firm. Large fruit, round. Very good quality. California origin.

62

6. **Formosa.** Fruit large, oval, greenish-yellow overlaid with red; flesh yellow; juicy. Tree tends to be a biennial bearer.

7. **Shiro.** Clear yellow skin and flesh. Good eating plum.

8. **Santa Rosa.** Dark reddish-purple, large, oblong, juicy. Fair quality.

9. **Abundance.** Red with yellow flesh, medium-sized fruit, round.

10. **Burbank.** The standard for late Japanese varieties. Fruit red with yellow flesh, medium-sized with firm flesh. Ripens unevenly requiring several pickings. Tree is low, wide-spreading and somewhat flat topped.

11. **Kelsey.** Very late, long season. Large, red, conical fruit. Good shipper. One of the first of the Japanese varieties introduced into the United States.

12. **Others.** Nubiana, Wickson, Duarte, Satsuma.

Native varieties

The American native plums have flesh and juice with a good flavor, but the astringency near the skin is objectionable. Some are extremely cold hardy. These types have been used in breeding plums for areas with severe winters. Examples of these varieties, in order of ripening — La Crescent, Underwood, Pipestone, Fiebring, Redglow, Superior, Toka, Elliott, Ember, Assiniboine.

The native varieties developed for the South include Wild Goose, Downing and Wayland. The Chicasaw plum has been successfully crossed with the Japanese type for use in the South and as far north as southern Ohio. Terrill and McRae are examples.

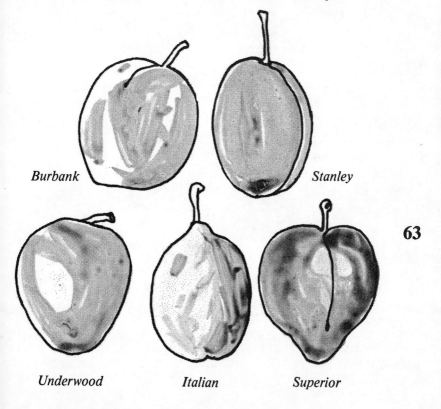

Burbank *Stanley*

Underwood *Italian* *Superior*

The Apricot

The apricot *(Prunus armeniaca),* like the peach, plum, and cherry, is a drupe fruit. Horticulturally, apricots are considerably smaller than commercial peaches, are bright orange-yellow with a red blush, have fine hairs or none at all, and have a distinctive flavor. The flesh is comparatively dry.

The largest commercial production is in California with a small amount in Washington, Utah, Colorado, Idaho and Oregon.

About 50% of the crop is dried, 25% is canned, and 25% is used for fresh fruit. Several varieties that have been developed are satisfactory for home orchards. You might find them beneficial for diversity and for possible roadside marketing.

The apricot is very susceptible to killing by early frost and attacks from diseases such as brown rot. This probably accounts for the lack of widespread planting, because apricots are very nutritious. The apricot contains 9 times as much Vitamin A as the average of 18 other common fruits and twice as much as its nearest competitor, the nectarine. It exceeds the average of these 18 fruits in protein, carbohydrates, phosphorus and niacin; it is slightly lower in fat, calcium, ascorbic acid and thiamine.

Plant breeders are beginning to work on test plantings that will broaden the growing areas.

Planning and Preparation

Temperature
The standard varieties require approximately 850 hours of below 45°F to break the rest period. Some of the Mediterranean types seem to have low chilling requirements and should be suitable for some of the southern climates.

Site location
The apricot grows best on a north slope that provides good air drainage. The north slope may retard the bud formation just enough to prevent damage from early spring frost. The apricot blooms earlier than peaches, and thus stands a greater risk of damage from spring frost.

Soil
The apricot prefers a deep sandy loam soil, but it will grow in heavier soils if ample moisture is present. The apricot is more shallow rooted than the apple and some of the other fruit trees; therefore, it cannot stand the competition of grass for moisture.

Planting
The apricot trees are commonly spaced 20 to 25 feet apart in all directions.

1. Dig the planting holes deep enough so that the tree can be set a little deeper than it grew in the nursery and large enough so that roots can be spread in the hole.

2. Remove all injured roots and any extremely long or unbalanced roots.
3. Spread the roots so that they will tend to grow in all directions. This will insure that later the tree will have firm anchorage. The apricot tree has shallow roots and will need a widely spread root system, not only for support, but to increase the area from which the tree can draw moisture and nutrients.
4. Use top soil to backfill around the roots.
5. Tamp the soil firmly around the roots. Be sure to eliminate the possibility of any air pockets.
6. Use water to settle the soil.
7. Be careful not to let the roots dry out during the planting.

Pruning and Thinning

Pruning at planting time

If possible use the branches to establish the framework for a modified leader system. Be sure to head-back enough to balance the root system. The apricot tree buds out early and new growth can tax the weakened root system before the new roots have a chance to take hold.

The branches of the apricot tree, though often heavier and larger than those of the peach, are inclined to become long and willowy unless they are headed-back to desirable laterals. In like manner, the trees become too thick unless a fair amount of thinning out is practiced.

Pruning a mature tree

As the trees become older, especially after several heavy crops, increase the amount of pruning in order to stimulate growth and increase fruit size. Prune to replace branches composed of older spurs with branches of younger spurs. Aim for 13 to 30 inches of shoot growth each year in young trees and 10 to 14 inches of growth in older trees. Do not allow the limbs to become unbranched and willowy.

The apricot trees often bear a few fruits at 3 to 4 years of age, but more often start production at 4 to 6 years. The life of a good orchard is 15 to 20 years.

Thinning a bearing tree

The growth stages of apricots are much the same as the peach. You can follow many of the same procedures, including hand thinning. Leave more fruit on the apricot tree than the peach tree because the apricot is a smaller size. You need to thin early biennial bearers, such as Blenheim and Tifton, in order to maintain as much of their annual bearing quality as possible.

Soil Management

Cultivation

Cultivate the orchard with a disk harrow in the late spring and summer. Apricots do not grow well in sod-managed orchards. The

67

Apricot Blossoms

competition with the grass during July, August, and September reduces the number of flower buds and slows the rate of bud development. Fruit set by the late-developing flowers are smaller than normal and mature 1 to 3 weeks later.

Cover crops
Cover crops are commonly used, but they are the type that can be planted in late September or October.

Mulching
If you live in the eastern regions where irrigation is not common, mulch under the trees.

Fertilizing
Since apricots are so similar in growth and fruiting to the peach, they generally require similar fertilizer treatments. The apricot tree responds to nitrogen and potassium with improved vigor, better bloom and increased yield. Phosphorus applied to the cover crop should be sufficient to meet the needs of the trees.

Apricot trees are more susceptible to zinc deficiencies than some of the other fruit trees. The typical symptoms are "little leaf" or "rosette." Zinc deficiencies can be corrected with foliage sprays during the early spring.

Harvesting
Harvest the crop as tree-ripe fruit. When harvested a little early, the fruit lacks flavor and dessert quality is unsatisfactory. Be careful with ripe fruit because it is susceptible to bruising and is very perishable.

Insects and Diseases
Most of the insects and diseases which attack the other drupe fruits also attack the apricot. In many cases, the *plum curculio* is the chief insect pest and brown rot the chief disease. A good spray schedule to fit the area is a must to control the *curculio* and brown rot if satisfactory fruit production is to be obtained.

Varieties

Check with the local state extension service for varieties of apricots best adapted to your area. Some of the newer varieties have been recently planted in the Midwest and East.

The leading commercial varieties include Royal, Tifton, Blenheim, Early Montgamet (a very large variety), Perfection, Stewart, and Chinese. A few of the more promising varieties are Early Orange, Wilson Delicious and Sunglo (from Utah).

The Siberian apricot is quite hardy, but is not grown commercially because of its small fruit. Now being used in test plantings and for crop breeding, it looks promising for the North Central States.

Some varieties for testing in the East are Alfred and Farmingdale (New York), Curtis and Goldcot (Michigan), Coffing (Indiana), Flaming Gold, Gold Kist, Patterson and Pinkerton (California). Moongold and Sungold were developed in Minnesota for areas where hardiness is very important. Others of the Siberian type are Sunshine, Anda, Manchu, Niguta, Sing, and Tola — all from South Dakota.

The Cherry

Cherries are a drupe fruit. Horticulturally, the two main types of cherries are sweet *(Prunus avium)* and pie, tart or sour *(Prunus cerasus)*. The term of pitted or pie cherry is used commercially, because the term sour is somewhat of a handicap in marketing.

The most concentrated growing areas for sweet cherries are in the Bay region of California, western Oregon, central Washington, and parts of Utah, Idaho, Colorado and Montana. Some are also raised around the Great Lakes region.

The most concentrated growing areas for sour cherries are in the eastern shore region of Lake Michigan, Door County Peninsula of Wisconsin, western New York, western Pennsylvania, northern Ohio and in Oregon, Washington, Colorado and Utah.

Cherries are very restrictive in their climate demands, being neither able to withstand extremely cold or hot weather. Essentially they are a cool-climate fruit and in the East do not succeed in commercial plantings south of the Ohio River. Cherries are also at the mercy of moisture conditions in both blooming and fruiting stages. Continued rain during bloom prevents proper setting of fruit. If much rain occurs at fruiting time, the firm, sweet cherry often cracks. On the other hand, cherries are very sensitive to drought. The growth of young trees can be seriously stunted by drought. Brown rot and other fungus diseases take heavy toll.

Planning and Preparation

Precipitation

Cherry trees require relatively heavy amounts of water during spring and early summer. New growth is made while the fruits are developing, and an adequate supply of moisture at this time is important. Cherries are very susceptible to "wet feet," so do not over water. Do not let the trees suffer from a deficiency during the late growth period after the crop has been picked.

Site location

The most favorable locations for cherry orchards are on hillsides near large bodies of water. Large lakes help to even out the temperature. Slopes help to provide drainage for both air and water.

Soil

An ideal soil for growing cherries is a well-drained, warm, deep, freeworking, gravely or sandy loam. It must be capable of holding moisture for two to three weeks during the period of high water use by the cherry trees. Cherries can't tolerate "wet feet." The soil must have good internal drainage.

Planting

Preparing to plant

The best time to plant cherry trees is in the early spring. The soil should be well prepared, preferably having been in cultivation for at least one year. Space the trees 20 feet x 25 feet or 25 feet x 25 feet. Losses are greater in planting time with cherries, particularly sweet cherries, than with most other fruits. The buds are easily rubbed off in handling. The buds open early in the spring, and the root system is slow to get started.

Tart cherry trees are usually planted as 2-year-old trees. Sweet cherries are usually planted as 1-year-old whips.

Planting the trees

1. Dig the holes by hand.
2. Cut off broken or injured roots. Don't expose the roots to sun and wind.
3. Set the trees slightly lower than they grew in the nursery.
4. Use top soil for backfill.
5. Tamp carefully around the roots to avoid any air pockets.
6. Use sufficient water at planting to settle the soil around the roots.

Pruning

Pruning at planting time

The trees should be pruned by heading-back 1-year-old trees to about 3 to 3½ feet. If the nurserymen trim the trees, that should be all the pruning the tree needs.

In the case of a 2-year-old tree, the top must be thinned. Remove whole branches rather than cut back branches severely. Balance the root system and top by some pruning so that the tree thrives in the first year after planting. Head back the selected scaffold just enough to obtain a well-shaped tree.

72

Pruning a bearing tree

Prune bearing trees to eliminate weak and unnecessary limbs, to open the center of the tree, and to keep the top fairly low. Pruning is also necessary to keep annual production of new wood at a suitable length.

Because of the persistent fruit-spur system, less renewal wood is needed than for most deciduous fruits. The annual terminal growth of upright wood in the top of bearing trees should average 8 to 12 inches long. Because pruning and nutrition satisfactorily regulate fruit size, thinning is not normally practiced.

Soil Management

Cultivation

If you raise cherries commercially, cultivate with a disk harrow during spring and early summer. Start as soon as the ground can be worked in the spring. Terminate cultivation in the latter part of early summer.

Cover crop

A cover crop is usually sown in late summer, or as soon as possible after the crop is harvested, to help prevent erosion and leaching. Sod alone in the cherry orchard is unsatisfactory as it uses too much moisture when the fruit crop is maturing.

Fertilizing

Soil and leaf analysis should determine fertilizer requirements for your cherry orchard. Normally, a good fertilizer program for the cover crops will suffice for the orchard. A small amount of nitrogen and potassium may be helpful if distributed directly under the trees. As a general rule, apply 0.05 pounds of actual nitrogen for each year of the tree's age.

Insects and Diseases

Since pest and disease controls vary in different areas, a good local spray schedule should be obtained from the county agent. One of the most dangerous pests is a cherry fruit fly that lays eggs in small slits in the fruit. The egg hatches into a whitish larva that has a curved body and a brown head. The *plum curculio* also attacks cherries.

Brown rot disease causes severe losses in cherries during hot, humid weather at harvest. Leaf spot is another disease that is most destructive to tart cherries.

Varieties

Sweet cherry varieties

There are two horticultural groups of sweet cherry varieties. The HEART group is characterized by soft, tender flesh and heart-shaped fruits. It includes dark colored varieties with reddish juice, and light colored varieties with near colorless juice. The BIGAR-REAU group is characterized by round fruit with firm, crisp, breaking flesh. This group includes dark red or black varieties, as well as light colored or yellowish ones.

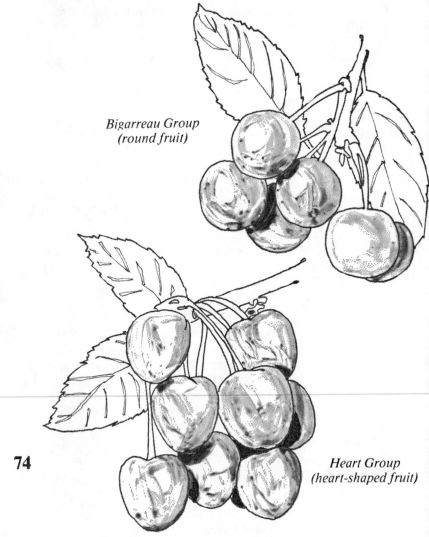

*Bigarreau Group
(round fruit)*

*Heart Group
(heart-shaped fruit)*

The list below presents the varieties in the order of their maturity. H is for Heart; B is for Bigarreau.

1. **Seneca** (H). Purplish-black, medium-sized, soft, juicy. Extreme earliness is its chief merit.

2. **Vista** (B). Larger, firmer, and more attractive than Black Tartarian.

3. **Black Tartarian** (H). Medium purplish-black, soft, juicy and rich. The leader of its group in the East.

4. **Venus** (B). Good size and quality, shiny black. Heavy cropper.

5. **Bing** (B). Dark red, black when fully ripe, large, firm, juicy, aromatic. Ships well, cracks in rainy season, excellent canner.

6. **Deacon** (B). Slightly smaller than the Bing. Highly resistant to cracking. Used as a pollinator in the West. Good canning quality.

7. **Napoleon** (B). The leading firm, light color variety. Well adapted to canning and for maraschino.

8. **Sue** (B). Not quite as large as Napoleon, but sweeter.

9. **Republican** (B). Dark red shipper. Used as a pollinator in the West.

10. **Van** (B). Good pollinator for Bing, Lambert and Napoleon, and vice versa. Fruit black, blacker than Bing. Medium size, more resistant to cracking than the Bing, good canner.

11. **Lambert** (B). Purplish red. Somewhat conical, cracks very badly in rainy weather. Sound fruit that ships well.

12. **Others.** Sam (B), Hedelfingen (B), Early Rivers (H), Lyons (H), Yellow Spanish (B), Emperor Francis (B), Schmidt (B), Sodus (B), Giant (B), Victor (B), Gil Peck (B).

Tart cherry varieties
As in sweet cherries, there are two horticultural groups. The AMARELLE group is characterized by light red flesh and juice. The MORELLO group is characterized by dwarf trees and late season ripening.

1. **Early Richmond** (A). Early, but has only fair size and quality. The tree is a little more hardy than Montmorency.

2. **Montmorency** (A). This is the only cherry of the tarts that is of commercial importance. Very widely grown. Is one of the very few that does well outside the normal cherry growing regions. It will tolerate more warm weather than most other varieties.

3. **English Morello.** Has dark fruits.

4. **Ostheim.** About the same as English Morello, except somewhat earlier.

Dwarf Fruit Trees

You should consider using dwarf fruit trees in your orchard, because they are more easily and economically pruned, sprayed, thinned, and harvested than standard trees. They usually come into fruiting at a much earlier age and fruit is easier to pick. These advantages more than compensate for the additional initial cost — due to their higher price and the desire to plant more dwarf trees per acre. Small trees require less space and, if not crowded too much, will produce a very high percentage of high quality fruit.

Dwarf apple and pear trees have been grown commercially in Europe for many years and are now widely available in the United States. The selection of varieties is much greater in apple trees than in pear, peach, plum, cherry, apricot and nectarine trees, but more of these fruits are becoming available as the demand for dwarf varieties increases. The nurseries have become aware of the increased interest in dwarf fruit trees and are now producing them in sufficient numbers to bring the cost down in line with the price of standard trees. The production of semidwarf fruit trees has also become widespread. This is an intermediate-size tree between the full-dwarf and the standard-size tree.

Rootstocks have been investigated more thoroughly for apples than for other fruits. The East Malling Fruit Research Station (East Malling, Kent, England) has done outstanding research in this field. The Station has a series of rootstocks that give different degrees of dwarfing for apple trees. The rootstocks are classified as very dwarfing, which produce very small trees that have to be supported, and semidwarfing, which produce trees between the dwarf and standard size.

A tree is identified at the nursery by variety, and the East Malling Roman Numeral is assigned to the rootstock on which the tree is grown. East Malling IX (EMIX) has been widely tested in this country, and is the best of the full dwarfing stocks. Because the tree is only 20 to 40% of standard size, most of the crop can be picked from the ground. The trees come into bearing very early, often in the second or third year after planting. A mature tree on EMIX may produce up to 2 bushels of apples, and because of the close planting possible (10 x 12 feet), the trees may give high yields per acre. Most trees on EMIX rootstock will require a support because the root system is comparatively small and tends to be brittle.

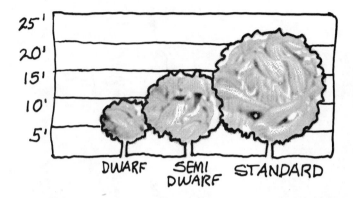

Planning and Preparation

The planting and care of dwarf fruit trees is much the same as the care of the standard size trees. Dwarf fruit trees are usually a year old when they are purchased from the nursery. They may be single stems, or may have two or three branches along the main stem. Plant in early spring in the north where winters are severe; in late fall or early spring in warmer climates.

Planting

Place full dwarf trees 10 to 12 feet apart each way, or 6 to 8 feet apart in rows that are 12 to 15 feet apart. For best results, plant dwarfs in soil that is moderately opened and well drained, not in fine-textured clay or in soil so coarse that it does not retain moisture. Because the dwarfs do not have as much root system as standard size trees, they will grow satisfactorily in soils that are not too deep. They do, however, require a good supply of moisture and may require irrigation when standard size trees could do without.

Plant dwarfs at the depth at which they stood in the nursery row, or a little higher. The point where the rootstock unites with the fruit variety should be above the ground. You can see a change in the bark color and, often, a slight curve in the trunk at this point.

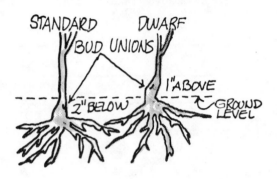

Pruning

Pruning at planting time

When setting out dwarf trees, prune them back to keep the tops in balance with the roots. A loss of roots always occurs in transplanting. If the trees are single stems 3 or 4 feet high, prune them back to about 30 inches. Generally, no further pruning is needed during the first year.

Pruning a growing tree

At the beginning of the second year of growth, keep 4 or 5 well-spaced branches and remove the balance. Trees to be grown as natural trees need no further pruning except to thin out branches. If you plan to train the tree on a trellis or wall, fasten branches to wires or to the wall during the first year. Remove new branches that form and grow upright. Cut them off to short stubs. This encourages spur-type growth.

Thinning a bearing tree

Dwarf fruit trees must be thinned of excess fruits. If not, they will set more fruit than they can develop to good size and quality. If the trees bear excess fruit, they may not bloom the next year.

Soil Management

Mulching is an excellent practice when growing dwarf fruit trees. Mulch of straw, grass clippings, or organic matter should be deep enough (3 or 4 inches) around each tree to smother grass and weeds. Keep the mulch a short distance away from the trunk, and hoe the ground immediately around the tree. This helps avoid attracting mice, as mice and rabbits damage trees by eating the bark and girdling the roots. If the trees are not mulched, hand hoe them to keep down grass and weeds within 3 to 4 feet of the trunk.

Fertilizing

After the trees start to grow in the spring, treat them with a fertilizer high in nitrogen. Scatter about 1 or 2 pounds about the tree from the trunk out. Use increasing amounts each year, applying in late fall and early spring. The mineral content of the soil must be maintained for dwarf trees.

Propagating Fruit Trees

If you are just starting out with fruit or nut trees, you will probably purchase your plant stock from a reliable nursery. At some point, however, you might want to experiment with propagation techniques. Budding and grafting are methods of propagating fruit and nut trees so that the trees reproduce true to form. Plants raised from seed seldom, if ever, reproduce fruit equal to the parent tree. Budding and grafting are the only sure way to know what the fruit from the tree will be. This is the way named varieties are reproduced.

Budding

Budding is one way to reproduce fruit and nut trees. With this method, a bud from a known variety is inserted into a seedling (or rootstock) of unknown quality. The rootstock is the vehicle through which the known variety will grow. Normally only one bud is inserted into each rootstock.

When to bud

Budding is usually done in the late summer or early fall when buds of the current season are well formed and the bark slips easily. Buds may be too immature, but seldom are they too mature for successful budding. The bud will start growth early the following spring.

Preparing the budsticks

Budsticks are the shoots of a known variety that carry the buds for budding. You should use the well-developed, plump and hard buds from the midportion of the shoot, discarding the soft tip buds and basal buds.

1. Cut shoots of the current season's growth from either bearing or nursery trees. Bearing trees are better since the quality of the fruit or nut is better.
2. Remove the leaves and keep the budstick moist after it has been cut from the parent tree. This will retard loss of moisture by evaporation from the leaves.

3. Use the buds as soon as possible; however, they can be kept for several days if they are wrapped in a moist cloth and placed in plastic bags.

Preparing the seedling

In early summer, prepare the seedling (rootstock) or limb that is to be budded by stripping off the lateral shoots on the lower 6 inches of the stem. Wipe the stock clean of soil particles near the point of bud insertion. The bud can be inserted by two different methods: the T-cut bud and the patch bud.

Preparing the T-cut bud

1. At budding time, make a T-cut in the bark of the rootstock 2 to 3 inches above the ground or on the limb where the bud is to be inserted.
2. Make the cut through the bark to cambium depth (not into the wood).
3. Some budders prefer to make the transverse cut first, about 1/3 around the stock or about 2 inches on the limb.
4. Then make a vertical cut upward to meet the transverse cut.
5. As the knife reaches the transverse cut, twist the knife blade to raise the edges of the bark just enough, without tearing, so that the bud may be easily inserted.
6. Other budders prefer to make the upward cut first, then the transverse cut.

Preparing the patch bud

The patch bud differs from the T-bud in that two transverse cuts are made parallel to each other about 1 inch apart. They are usually made with a special knife that has the two blades a set distance apart to make both cuts at the same time.

1. Make the horizontal cut with the two-bladed knife.
2. Make the verticle cut from one parallel cut to the other.
3. Twist the knife slightly so the bark is raised.
4. Then slip the bud under the slit and trim off the excess.

81

Cutting the bud

When you cut the bud from the budstick, leave a shield below the bud to help hold the bud in place when it is inserted into the rootstock.

1. Hold the budstick by the top end with the lower end away from the body.
2. Place the knife 1/2 inch below the first suitable bud. With a shallow slicing movement, pass the knife beneath the bud approaching the surface 1 inch above it. The part around the bud will be the shield.

3. Cut the shield bearing the bud fairly thin, but not so thin that the soft growing tissue beneath the bark and wood is injured.
4. Retain the thin strip of wood that was cut with the shield.

Inserting the bud
1. After cutting, hold the bud by the petiole between the finger and thumb.
2. Insert the bud into the T-shape or the patch cut incision. Fast nurserymen that are experienced slip the bud on the knife directly into the cut. A properly inserted bud is at least 3/4 inch below the top transverse cut. Avoid undue manipulation or prying of the bark flaps.
3. Place the buds on the same side as the prevailing winds to prevent subsequent breakage.

Tying the bud
When the cambial layers are in close contact, they establish an intimate contact of the cambial region, usually producing thin-walled parenchyma cells that lead to interlocking cells, thus closing or briding the bud to the stock. Tying the bud to the rootstock will insure close contact.
1. After inserting the bud, wrap it snuggly. Rubber budding strips have largely replaced raffia or string. Rubber strips have the merit of expanding with growth of the rootstock. After exposure to the sun for a month or so, they will rot and fall off. By this time, a good union between bud and rootstock has taken place.
2. Be sure to leave the bud exposed.
3. Wrapping may be done either downward or upward. Pull the free end of the rubber strip under the last turn to hold it in place.

82

Caring after budding
The first indication you will have that the bud has united with the stock is that the leaf stem will drop off. In successful budding, the bud usually will have grown to the stock in 2 to 3 weeks. Shriveled adhering leaf stems often indicate failure. If the bark still separates readily from the wood, a new bud may be inserted in a new location on the stock.

Buds inserted in late July or later remain dormant until the following spring. Buds properly united with the stock do not require any winter protection such as banking soil around the budded stock. This eliminates two extra time-consuming operations, name-

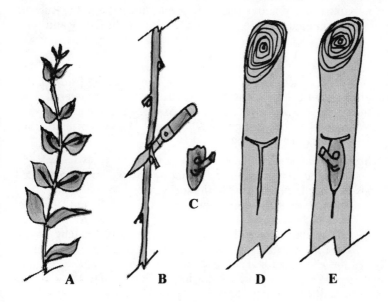

T-Budding

A *Source of buds*

B *Cutting the bud*

C *The shield bud*

D *T-cut in the stock*

E *Bud in place*

F *Bud tied in stock*

G *The branch cut off the stock the following spring*

83

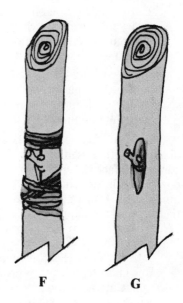

ly covering in the fall and uncovering in the spring. Cut off root-stock immediately above the grafted bud in early spring. Rub off all suckers that appear on the rootstock during the spring and early summer.

Grafting

To reproduce fruit or nut trees by grafting, the trunk of the seedling is cut off a few inches from the ground and material from a known variety is joined to it by one of the grafting methods, such as whip-and-tongue graft or four-flap graft. This is normally done in late winter or early spring.

Whip-and-tongue graft

This type of propagating is done in the winter. The grafted stock is transplanted in rows in the spring.

1. Use 1-year-old wood that is smooth, straight and free from branches.
2. The diameters of the stock and scion should match.
3. From about 2 inches above the basal end of the scion, make a diagonal cut to the base.
4. Make the tongue by cutting straight about 1-1/4 inches half way along the cut surface. Make the cut toward the apical end of the scion.
5. Make similar cuts on the rootstock.
6. Interlock the scion and the rootstock so that the cambium layers make as much contact as possible.
7. Secure the graft union with rubber tape or waxed string and wrap the graft with foil and plastic.

Four-flap graft

This method has become increasingly popular. It can be used successfully on fruit or nut trees to change the variety or to get a pollinator limb on the tree.

The four-flap graft method allows the use of wood twice the diameter of that used in the whip-and-tongue graft. The four-flap's contact surface is much greater than others. The surface is entirely covered with the bark flaps to facilitate fast healing and a strong union. The four-flap graft does not require any close fits and, therefore, is a good graft for beginners. Although the graft works better if the scion and the stock are the same size, the graft can be made with wood 25% larger or smaller.

1. Collect the scion wood in February. Collect vigorous, mature, last year's growth.
2. Cut the wood into lengths of approximately 20 inches. Each length will make three grafts.
3. Dip the scion wood in water and sling out the excess.

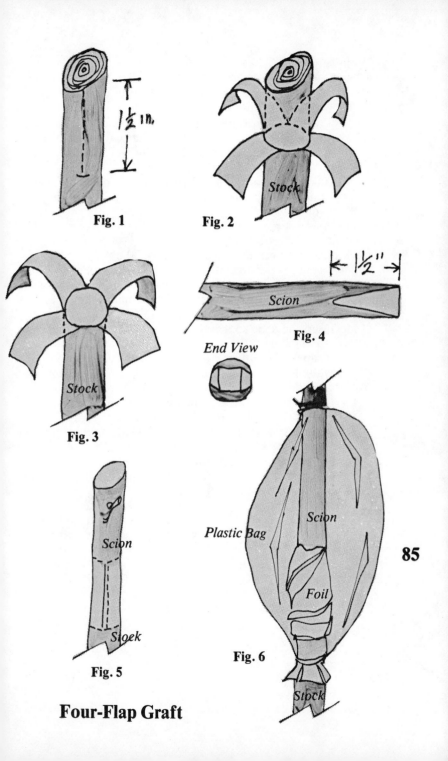

Fig. 1

Fig. 2

Stock

Fig. 3

Stock

$1\frac{1}{2}$ in.

$1\frac{1}{2}''$

Scion

Fig. 4

End View

Fig. 5

Scion

Stock

Plastic Bag

Scion

Foil

Stock

Fig. 6

85

Four-Flap Graft

4. Wrap in dry, new paper and plastic.

5. Store in a cool place (32°-35°F) such as a crisper in a refrigerator. Scion wood up to 1 inch in diameter can be used satisfactorily.

6. When you are ready to graft the scion wood to the rootstock, cut off the stock with a sharp knife or pruning shear at a point where the graft can be easily made. The stock should be about the same size as the scion.

7. Make 4 vertical cuts 1-1/2 inches long and equally spaced around the circumference of the stock. Make the cuts through the bark.

8. Pull back the bark forming 4 flaps. This will expose 1-1/2 inches of the stock.

9. Use sharp pruning shears to cut off the "plug." Be careful not to cut or damage the 4 flaps.

10. Use a sharp knife to cut the scion on 4 sides. Start the cut 1-1/2 inches from the end. Cut just under the bark. The end view will be square.

11. Insert the scion so that the 4 flaps will cover the 4 surfaces of the scion.

12. Wrap with plastic grafting tape or rubber tape. Leave the lower 1/4 inch of the graft exposed so that bleeding can drain out.

13. Cover the tape with aluminum foil. Then cover the entire graft with a plastic bag. Tie 1 inch below the foil.

14. After 3 or 4 weeks, growth should start. At this time, cut the plastic bag and pull it down to expose the scion.

15. Tie it 1 inch above the foil.

16. Three or four weeks later, remove the plastic, the plastic bag and foil and cut the tape.

17. Replace the foil to offer some protection for the graft. Tape again over the foil to keep the wind from blowing the graft out. The foil will compress a little to let the union grow.

18. Remove tape and foil in about a month. Remove the other growth on the stock when grafting and keep it in check during the growing season.

Beekeeping

Since bees play such an important role in pollinating fruit trees, anyone planning or maintaining an orchard should have bees available. In addition to their value as pollinators, bees produce delicious fresh honey and also provide fascinating social behavioral patterns for observation. Fresh honey can contribute to your family's diet as well as make an excellent addition to a roadside market.

If you don't want to get involved in a beekeeping operation, you might have a neighbor with bees who may be willing to place a colony or two close to your orchard so that you will get the benefit of the bees as pollinators while he enjoys the other benefits. However, before making up your mind, read the following information on beekeeping to give you a better idea of what is involved.

Members of the Hive

Honeybees are social insects. This means that they live together in a colony and depend on each other for survival. Most of the bees in a colony are workers (sterile females). Some are drones (males), whose only function is to mate with the queen.

DRONE   QUEEN   WORKER

Most of the time the hive will have only one queen. She is the only fertile female and lays the eggs to maintain or increase the colony. The queen bee normally flies from the hive when she is about a week old and mates in the air with several drones. When she returns to the hive, she begins to lay eggs. During her lifetime, she lays thousands of eggs, as many as a thousand a day. Each egg is layed in a separate cell of the honeycomb. Three days later the egg hatches into a larva. Worker bees feed and care for the larva for 6 days. They then seal the cell and 15 days later the young bee chews its way out.

Worker bees number up to about 60 thousand, depending on the egg laying ability of the colony queen, the space available and the food supply. The worker bees, who live about 6 weeks, collect food and water for the entire hive and guard against intruders. They also do all the housework including "air conditioning" the hive to maintain a constant temperature and humidity.

The number of drones (males) in a colony varies with the season of the year. There may be none in the winter, but several hundred during the summer. They are usually run out of the hive in the fall to save food for the workers.

BEEHIVE

Equipment

The basic equipment needed to begin a beekeeping operation should cost $50.00 or $60.00 and include the following items:

1. Hive to house bees
2. Frames and foundation to support the honeycombs in which the bees will store honey and raise young bees
3. Smoker to blow smoke into the hive to pacify the bees

while you're working with them

4. Hive tool with which to pry frames apart to examine the hive and harvest the honey
5. Veil to protect the face and neck from bee stings
6. Gloves to protect hands
7. Feeders to dispense sugar syrup until bees can produce their own food

If you plan to build the hive yourself, use a factory-made hive as a pattern. Reproduce all parts exactly so that all parts will fit together well and will be interchangeable with like parts from other hives.

Raising Bees

When to start

The best time to start beekeeping is in the springtime. Fruit trees and flowers are in bloom then and provide a good supply of nectar and pollen for the new colony. The hive should be assembled and ready to house the bees before they are purchased. Usually a two or three pound package of bees, with a queen, will be sufficient for a good start. Be sure that the bees are certified to be disease-free. Provide the new bees with a mixture of 50% sugar and 50% water. The syrup should be put in the feeder at the entrance to the beehive. The syrup will supply food to the bees until they are able to make and store their own honey.

Placing the hive

Locate the hive away from people to eliminate the possibility of someone being stung by the bees. In the warm, sunny climates, place the hive in the shade. In areas with extended periods of freezing temperatures, expose the hive to the sun and protect it from prevailing winds. Be sure to have a supply of good fresh water close by.

How bees live

The bees need four basic materials: nectar, pollen, propolis and water. They make honey out of nectar and use pollen to make beebread (food for young bees). They use propolis (a gummy substance collected from buds and injured tree parts) to seal cracks and waterproof their hive. They use the water to dilute the honey before eating it and to "air condition" their hive.

Bees cannot make honey without nectar, the sugary liquid substance produced by flowers. It is the raw material of honey and bees' main source of food. The color and flavor of honey depends on the kinds of plants from which the bees collect the nectar. Honey may be almost white, amber, or even reddish; its flavor can range from very mild to strong. Some plants will produce a particular flavor and color. Often the honey made from the nectar of that plant will be sold at a premium, such as sweet clover honey, alfalfa honey, citrus fruit honey and cotton honey.

As worker bees gather nectar from flowers, tiny particles of pollen stick to their bodies and accumulate in small balls on their hind legs. As this pollen is carried into the hives, the workers store it in the comb as "beebread." Later, worker bees in the hive consume the "beebread"; the nutrients in it are converted into larva food by special glands in the heads of nursebees. If a larva is selected to become a queen bee, that larva is fed extra rations containing enriched larva food called "royal jelly."

The average size colony of bees uses approximately 100 pounds of pollen each year. It is, therefore, important to locate the colony near a source of flowers, trees and grasses that are good sources of pollen.

The bees manufacture honeycomb from beeswax, which begins as a liquid made by glands on the underside of the workers' abdomens. As it is produced, the beeswax hardens into tiny wax scales. The workers use this wax to form the honeycomb, which in turn stores the nectar after the bees have evaporated most of the water from it. As the water evaporates, enzymes change the nectar into honey, and the bees seal it into the beeswax honeycomb.

Beekeepers often provide the bees with a foundation for the honeycomb. This foundation fits into hive frames and enables bees to speed up comb construction and provides a pattern for building a straight and easy-to-remove honeycomb. Some beekeepers produce comb honey by cutting out pieces of honeycomb, putting them in glass jars, and then filling the remaining space with liquid honey.

Another method of producing comb honey is to place small wooden boxes in the top of the hive just as the honey flow starts. The bees will fill the box with sections of honey, usually about a pound in each one. The majority of honey is extracted from the honeycomb and kept or sold as strained honey. The frame with the wax honeycomb is replaced in the hive to be used again by the bees.

Moving the colony

Occasionally you may need to move the bee colony from one location to another. Be sure to move it several miles away or the bees will find their way back to their old location. One method is to move the hive several miles away for a week or more and then relocate it to the new site. An alternate method is to move the hive a few feet each day until it reaches the new location.

Don't move the bees during the period of honey production. Night is the best time to move the hive, when all bees are inside. When making the move, cover the entrance with a screen. Do not seal the entrance tight or the bees may suffocate. Tie the hive together in advance to prevent it from coming apart during the move.

Enlarging the colony

As the bee colony grows, it will need more room. If the bees become too crowded and there isn't enough room for expansion of the brood-rearing area, they will swarm (fly off in large numbers, along with a queen, to start a new colony). Loss of a swarm of bees may leave the remaining colony weak and unable to store surplus honey.

To make room for more bees, add extra boxes of combs (supers) to the existing hive or onto the supers already in place. Always leave plenty of honey for the bees when harvesting. Only remove the amount that is estimated to be surplus to their needs. Be sure there is at least 50 pounds of honey in the hive when winter begins; otherwise, the bees may starve before spring.

Working with bees

The bees defend their honey supply with the only weapon they have — their sting. Try to work the bees when they are flying actively in favorable weather. Wear protective clothing — a veil over the head and face, gloves and close-woven, light colored clothing that fits tight at the wrists and ankles.

Always use a smoker when working the bees. Direct the smoke into the hive entrance before disturbing the bees. As the hive cover, or super, is removed, apply smoke gently to the exposed bees. Do not over-smoke.

If stung, remove the stinger immediately by scraping if off with a straight edged instrument or fingernail. Most beekeepers eventually develop an immunity to stings. However, if you develop an allergy to stings let someone else take care of the bees or don't have them around.

Varieties

In the United States, the Italian strain of bees is the most common. The Italian strain is hardy, industrious and relatively gentle. They are yellow or brown in color.

The caucasian strain is also widely kept. They are more gentle in nature than Italian bees. The caucasian bees are grey to black in color.

Some specially bred hybrid bees (crosses between two strains of bees) are available. They are usually more productive than standard strains, but after a year or two, the offspring they produce may bear no resemblance to the original hybrid bees. If you should decide to keep hybrid bees, it is a good idea to replace the queen each year. This will help to assure a uniformly strong colony.

Diseases

The honeybee is subject to several diseases, none of which are dangerous to people. Specific information on bee diseases or pests can be obtained from your local county agent. The Superintendent of Documents, U.S. Printing Office has for sale a booklet entitled "Diagnosing Bee Diseases in the Apiary". The number of this booklet as A1B313, and the cost is 15¢. It also has a booklet on "Controlling the Greater Wax Moth." The number is FB2217, and it costs 10¢.

Agricultural Handbook No. 335, "Bee Keeping in the United States," gives complete information on all phases of beekeeping, and would be most beneficial to you if, at this point, you have decided to become a beekeeper. It can be obtained from the Superintendent of Documents, U.S. Government Printing Office, Washington, D.C., 20402, and the cost is $1.00.

Glossary

Air drainage
Movement of cold air through the trees and away from them.
Biennial plants
Plants that require two years to complete their growth cycle. Some trees and plants that produce a crop only every other year are known as biennial bearers.
Botany
The study of plant growth.
Budding
Propagating a good variety of fruit onto an unknown or inferior rootstock by slipping an inactive bud from a known variety onto the rootstock.
Chilling hours
The number of hours that the temperature must remain below 45°F to provide a rest period and thus enable a variety to produce fruit.
Cover crops
Crops planted between the trees to furnish protection to the bare ground.
Cross-unfruitful
Trees that must be pollinated by a like variety; will not cross with other varieties.
Culls
An inferior developed fruit.
Cultivation
Plowing or disking the soil between the trees.
Deciduous plants
Plants that require a rest period in the winter, shed their leaves and put out new growth in the spring.
Dormant
A period during the winter when the tree is at rest.
Grafting
A method of reproducing a known variety of fruit by joining the growth of the known variety onto a rootstock of another variety.

Head-back
Cutting back long limbs.
Heeling-in
Setting young plants in the soil temporarily until they can be transplanted in the field.
Herbicides
Chemicals used to control weeds and undesirable plants.
Irrigation
A method of applying water to plants to supplement rainfall.
Laterals
The extension of several branches from the trunk.
Mulching
Applying hay, straw, leaves and other such material to the soil around a tree or plant.
Propagating
A method of reproducing trees or plants.
Pruning
Removing unwanted or unneeded parts of a plant.
Rootstock
The part of a tree below where the bud or graft is made.
Scaffold limb
A main limb growing from the trunk of a tree.
Self-unfruitful
A tree that requires pollen from another variety to be able to set fruit.
Sod system
Raising fruit trees in a grassy area and not plowing or cultivating the area.
Spurs
The small growths where the fruit is borne on the tree.
Subsoil
The material under the top soil. Usually clay, gravel, etc.
Terminal growth

The ends of the limbs that were produced during the current season's growth.
Thinning
Removing fruit that is in excess of what the tree can normally be expected to mature.
Top soil
The soil on the top of the ground that has organic matter and minerals and in which roots will readily grow.
Watersprouts
Shoots that develop around the base and lower trunk of the tree.
Whip
A seedling that has not developed any branches.

Countryside Gardening Books
Little Book Series
5½ by 8 inch format

INDOOR ASSORTMENT

Cactus & Succulents (101)
Herb Gardening (102)
Foliage Houseplants (103)
Flowering Houseplants (104)
Vines & Ivy (106)
Ferns & Palms (107)
African Violets (108)
Orchids (111)
Houseplant Handcrafts (114)
Houseplant Multiplying (117)
Don't Throw it Away . . . Plant it (118)
Houseplant RX (119)
Greenhouse Gardening (126)

OUTDOOR ASSORTMENT

Container Planting (105)
Geraniums (109)
Begonias (110)
Garden Bulbs (112)
Correct Planting Methods (113)
Vegetable Gardening (115)
Entice Birds to Your Garden (116)
Shade Trees (120)
Evergreens (121)
Groundcovers, Vines & Hedges (122)
Annuals & Perennials (123)
Better Lawns (124)
Rose Handbook (125)

Large Books
8¼ by 10½ inch format

SIX WAYS TO GROW HOUSEPLANTS, (201)
   by Muriel Orans, 265 color photos, **$3.95**
NEW IDEAS IN FLOWER GARDENING, (202)
   by Derek Fell, 225 color photos, **$3.95**
LOOK, MOM, IT'S GROWING, (203)
   by Ed Fink, illustrated children's book, **$2.95**
HOUSEPLANTS AND INDOOR LANDSCAPING, (204)
   by Muriel Orans, 248 color photos, **$3.95**
HOW TO PLANT A VEGETABLE GARDEN, (205)
   by Derek Fell, 100 color photos, **$3.95**
HOME LANDSCAPING, (206)
   over 500 color photos, **$5.95**
BONSAI AND THE JAPANESE GARDEN, (207)
   by Domoto & Kay, 85 color photos, **$3.95**
RAISE VEGETABLES, FRUITS & HERBS IN CONTAINERS, (208)
   by "Doc" & Katy Abraham, **$2.95**

95

A full color brochure describing all Countryside books on gardening
as well as other subjects is available on request.

Countryside
Books

A. B. Morse Co.
200 James St., Barrington, Ill. 60010

5/82